D1172874

Naked Civics

Naked Civics: Strip Away the Politics to Build a Better World

Copyright © 2012 by Nate Garvis

Editor: Diane O'Connell
Cover Design: George Foster and Spunk Design Machine
Interior Design: David Moratto

Library of Congress Control Number: 2012908062

Library of Congress Cataloging-in-Publication Data has been applied for.

ISBN: 978-0-9855926-0-8

First Edition
Printed in the United States of America

www.nakedcivics.com
Naked Civics ©

Strip Away the Politics to Build a Better World

NATE GARVIS

with GENE REBECK

For my beautiful daughters Ivy and Violet.

This is a great world that will be made better
by what you will do in it.

CONTENTS

Contents

The Honor Roll

TO BE A GOOD TEACHER IS TO FIRST be a good student. I can't claim to be a good teacher, but I can say that over the years, I've tried to be a good student, a thirsty student and an appreciative student. And in that vein of appreciation, I'd like to thank just a few of my teachers. Yes it's trite to say, but I hope forgivable because of its truth: There are just too many people to thank for the experiences that led to writing on a subject that I've had a deep passion for throughout my entire adult life.

Tom Wiese is a lifelong friend, my business partner, and one of the wisest people I've ever met. His sage guidance throughout this project has been immeasurably valuable. Tom also has a killer sense of humor and possesses a personality that exudes mirth and generosity. If alignment of dreams and visions undergirded by complete trust is the most important currency these days, then I have an extremely wealthy relationship with my pal Tom. Journeying with you, my friend, is one of the greatest joys of my life.

As you'll see, my professional path of being a civic designer began at Dayton Hudson and Target. I had an enormously satisfying career there, and I am gratified that I continue that relationship today. As is always the case, an institution is only as great as its people. And I can tell you that the place is rife with great talent and I have been graced by so many who have served as mentors, friends, and collaborators over the years. Susan Flack, who has served as Target's outside government affairs counsel for decades, has been an important and valuable source of support over the years to me. We have traveled the world together and explored ideas throughout it all. She's truly one of a kind.

Jim Hale, the company's former General Counsel, gave me the overt permission to focus on community health from day one. Honestly, is that really what you would expect from a Fortune Fifty top tier corporate officer? From my perspective, you just can't give a young and very inexperienced public affairs executive a better gift. And what is just as remarkable, is that gift was only extended by Tim Baer, who became Target's General Counsel after Jim's retirement. What Jim allowed me to plan and start, Tim became a critical backer of and the producer of what we were able to scale together. Both are true blue friends and two of the finest people I've ever known personally and professionally.

Jodee Kozlak is another former colleague of mine. As Target's head of Human Resources, she has been the main architect of my career transition and words cannot adequately describe my appreciation for her friendship, counsel, and partnership. An incredibly exciting thinker, Jodee has been instrumental in creating new opportunities for me to push the envelope. She's just one of the coolest people I've ever known. If you could ever ascribe the word "benefactors" to a professional path like mine, Jodee and Tim would fit that bill. Both are class acts with big brains and even bigger hearts. Their wisdom, continued support, and friendship are treasured, and I'm truly grateful for their faith in my efforts over the years.

Throughout my travels in the world of public affairs, my friend Doug Pinkham has been a constant and greatly valued thought partner. As President of the esteemed Public Affairs Council, Doug has been at the forefront of some of the most important global public policy conversations over the years. He treads with deep wisdom and a true concern for the public affairs profession and its impact on our communities. And the proof? Can you name another Washington DC-based trade association that can lay claim to memberships from Chevron to the Mayo Clinic? When it comes to operating at the highest public standard and asking the best from this influential community, Doug sets the bar and he does it with incredible wit, intelligence, and wisdom. There are few people whom I'd rather talk with in terms of what is, what should be, and how we're going to get there.

Since leaving that terrific gig at Target, my work with Babson College has given me tremendous excitement. A quick word on Babson: From the time when folks first started creating rankings for entrepreneurial education, Babson's been at the top of the heap, listed right there as number one. Always. And I believe that the reason for their recognized excellence is that this crowd believes that entrepreneurialism isn't merely a business practice, but rather, it's a problem-solving mind-set that can be taught and can apply anywhere when faced with an ambiguous, quickly changing environment — in other words, a world that looks a lot like today. My dear friend and even dearer soul mate, Cheryl Kiser, serves as the Executive Director of the Lewis Institute and the Social Innovation Lab at the school, and has graciously allowed me to play in her sandbox. I am quite certain that I've never met someone who is more connected to more interesting and impactful people than Cheryl. And I never have doubts as to why that is the case. To stand next to Cheryl is to be next to a powerfully beating heart that spreads infectious optimism and purpose to actually do what your dreams tell you. I cherish every single moment with her.

Like Tom Wiese mentioned above, there is another couple of childhood friends whom I'd like to throw into this mix. Jim Sachs, on paper, is my ten-months older first cousin, but in reality, he's my older brother. And there are birthday party photos going back to fourth grade with my friend Rich Paisner and me, although it wasn't until the ripe old age of twelve when we really started getting into trouble together. Throughout the year, we have great conversations, but once a year, the three of us travel to the northern woods of Minnesota to take a "boys' weekend" at the Sachs family cabin. Those weekends have been tremendously helpful in terms of testing out my thinking on a couple of wise and trusted friends. And I swear that it would have happened without many of those conversations fueled by fine Scotch. But it helped.

For many years, I have benefited from the partnership and friendship of Sean Kershaw, who leads what, unfortunately, is a rare organization in our country: a citizens' led public policy think tank. The Citizens League is an amazing outfit that has benefited me personally and benefited my community over and over again. They've had some pretty terrific leaders over the years, but I'd be hard pressed to think of anyone better than Sean. He's smart, he's witty, he's generous of mind and spirit, and I get to call him my friend.

Karen Antebi has grown into yet another trusted and dear friend, who always continues to impress me with her powerful and deep thinking. As Mexico's Counselor for Economic Affairs based in Washington, DC, Karen became part of the landscape of my many trips to the nation's capital throughout the years. In this new life of mine, those trips are not as plentiful, but our friendship has remained unabated. Full of wise perspective and overt intelligence with a passion for things that matter, Karen has honed and shaped so much of my thinking through our many wonderful conversations over the years. There are lots of colors that I could ascribe to Karen, but beige isn't one of them. She's a spark of bright colors that leave lasting impressions.

There are two people who helped me write this book, one mentioned on the cover, the other not. Kolina Cicero has been just the greatest sidekick I could hope for. She helps me scout for interesting things to think about, to design around, and to write about. Together, we produce my blog, and plenty of that work has ended up within these pages. And then, there's Gene Rebeck. Gene is listed on the cover as the person who helped me produce the words you will read. And he did a fine job of that. I originally engaged him, knowing that I didn't have the discipline nor would devote the time to write a book. But what happened turned out to be a much more important part of the "what" this book is all about. The real purpose of this work is to share some thoughts and start a conversation. Well, what better way to do that than produce a book out of a conversation? Gene has been so much more than a recorder, so much more than a scribe. It would be hard for me to adequately describe how enjoyable all those many conversations, give and take of ideas, and sharing of perspectives were. But I can describe to you that this book wouldn't look nor feel nearly like it does had I not had the able partnership of my friend Gene.

And in that very same vein of outing me as the rookie author that I am, I want to thank my book design and editorial team. "Lost in the woods" would be a fair description of me without this incredibly talented trio. George Foster, award winning book cover designer extraordinaire, absolutely shocked me by how easily he and I fell into the same vibe about the subject matter of this book. Within two or three iterations, he nailed it with his artistry. My friends over at Spunk Design Machine, who are responsible for designing other elements such as the web site, then augmented George's work in wonderful fashion. Together, they have produced an identity that expresses the stripping away of old notions that prevent us from moving forward in today's world. I'm incredibly grateful for their talents.And pivoting into the talents of my interior designer David Moratto was equally thrilling. David took George's work and crafted interior architecture that not only built upon George's artistic foundation, but also expanded it so that I could create four separate but interrelated elements throughout this work. What these two design talents created pleases me well beyond what I could have expected. And each and every conversation with the two of them was a deeply satisfying pleasure.

Diane O'Connell has served as my trusted editor and wise teacher as this book went from raw manuscript into book form. I can't thank her enough for effectively challenging me to pull even more clarity out of my thoughts, for ensuring that I remain true to the aim and intention behind this work and for guiding me through this new experience. Throughout it all, she has always treated me with such a warm and gentle touch. It would have been so easy for someone else to say something like "Are you kidding? How green are you at this?" but Diane has never taken the bait. And I think I threw some pretty nice bait out there! Thank you for the many wonderful discussions about the subject matter within *Naked Civics* and thank you for giving this project your all. I am eternally grateful.

A guy has to thank his parents, doesn't he? Well I do, but trust me it's for a whole lot more than "thanks for tolerating me enough to allow me to reach adulthood." Both of my parents have given me specific and important perspectives and skills that hopefully you will pick up on in the ensuing pages. My mother, Audra Keller, comes from a long line of civic actors. Her dad, Nate (whom I never knew but was named after), her mother Mollie and her grandfather Adolf, were all active and involved citizens in the best sense. They made things happen. They supported important people in our communities and, in turn, they became important. They happened to life, life did not happen to them, just like my mom. And she can rightfully claim responsibility for instilling in me the importance of community concern and involvement. There were a lot of things my mom probably hoped I'd become, but a spectator wasn't one of them, and she was pretty damn clear about that.

My dad, Allan Garvis, also instilled in me a couple of things that have become instrumental to how I go about my work and life. The first is a love of all types of people. My dad digs just about everyone. His tolerance and appreciation for those in all walks of life has always been an important part of how I want to see myself. What a gift it is to have a model for that kind of behavior in someone like your dad. The other thing you should know about my dad is that he has a very sick sense of humor. You don't want to sit next to him at a funeral. Trust me. What I've learned from him is that humor is a greatly underappreciated tool in our society. It allows you to weather storms without getting shipwrecked. But more importantly, it allows you to address uncomfortable issues with a humanity that takes away a lot of the sting. There are few people who allow me to laugh through life like my dad.

And last, but hardly the least, I want to share with you my love and appreciation for my tiny wife Trissa. At five feet tall dripping wet, she doesn't mind me calling her "tiny wife" because she is a huge person in a beautiful and petite package. Here's what I want you to know about my wife: She's interesting and interested in so many things, she's quick and smart, and she reads people and situations with alarming speed and accuracy. Here's what she needs to hear from me: I love you and I'm blessed to have you in my life. Thanks for making just about everything worthwhile.

So, that is it! This is an uncomfortably incomplete list, but my thanks and appreciation for the people above are presented with deep and true feelings. What you see in your hands just simply wouldn't be there as it is without their presence in my life.

Introduction

A NUMBER OF YEARS AGO, I GAVE A speech with the pithy title: Uncivil Discourse and the Rise of the Outrage Industry. The premise was that we were living in an environment where we had actually begun to commoditize anger. People were selling it in packaged form, we were buying it by the hours, and it wasn't good for us. At the end, I took some Q & A and a very good friend of mine named Ed Driscoll raised his hand and said exactly this: "Nice speech. So, what?" Honestly … from a friend! But what he was actually saying, and we had a good laugh about it right then and there by the way, was that now that we're aware of the challenges of living in constant anger, what should we do about it? Well, Ed, it took about a half dozen years, but here's your answer.

What if I told you that *how* we address the many challenges facing our communities is the biggest and most important challenge of all? In *Naked Civics*, I'm going to show you why that is the case. We are about to start a conversation on how to create a better community by thinking beyond our angry politics. In this book, you'll not only learn about the tools that we have at our disposal, but you'll see how they can be used to create new ways — new *designs* — to also make our communities more prosperous, and not just economically. You'll also see how you can participate in this work and how you can find it inspiring — even fun. Yes ... I said it: fun. It's time to start getting serious about fun and getting back into that engaging space. Because what personally inspires and motivates you to make things better is a critical element of getting beyond our current environment of anger, political polarity, doom, and despair.

In other words, this book is about how we can think creatively and collaboratively as we move into our future. And this, in turn, can help us overcome our toxic political climate. Yes, this is an optimistic vision of our common future. But I know from my own experience that it's also a very practical one.

Ironically, my journey on this path, one that fills me with such optimism and even joy, started with a very nasty crime.

A Murder

In May 1999, a repeatedly-convicted sex offender named Donald Blom was out on the streets of a small town in western Minnesota. He abducted, raped, and murdered a nineteen-year-old girl named Katie Poirier. It was a horrendous crime that shook that small community, indeed my entire home state of Minnesota, to the bone. Blom later confessed to the crime, and he is now behind bars for the rest of his life. That crime changed my life, too. From 1993 to 2010, I worked for Dayton-Hudson, now known as Target Corporation. Public policy and politics were the center of my professional attention, and when you work for a publicly-facing and community-oriented retailer like Target, you have permission to think about a whole host of issues that make a community prosperous enough to support you. It was a great gig with a great company.

In 1999, Jesse Ventura, Minnesota's first and (so far) only governor belonging to the Independence Party, was wise enough to choose a very smart man, former county attorney and former state legislator Charlie Weaver, to serve as his Commissioner of Public Safety. During a conversation, I asked Charlie, who is also a longtime friend of mine, why Donald Blom had been out on the streets. Charlie's answer shocked me: At that time, Minnesota had some eleven hundred-plus criminal justice jurisdictions, from the beat cop to the sentencing judge, and they didn't share information very effectively. Some smaller cities were actually keeping fingerprints in shoeboxes. Put another way: There were plenty of cracks in the way our law enforcement system was designed for Blom to slip through.

"Target knows where every pair of socks is in its inventory," I replied to Charlie. "Yet, Minnesota doesn't know where all of its felons are." That conversation marked the beginning of a partnership between Target, Charlie's office, and a couple of Minnesota legislators, Democratic Senator Jane Ranum and Republican House member Rich Stanek. Together, they led the state in a bipartisan effort to create an information-sharing network called CriMNet. Today, we bemoan the lack of bipartisanship. Well, this was tripartisanship. And everyone worked well with each other. But even more importantly, the product that was created through the many partnerships that became CriMNet brought value to our community. It is a herculean task to integrate all the data points that make up a criminal justice system, and according the state's Bureau of Criminal Apprehension (where CriMNet is housed), the state's myriad of jurisdictions are much more coordinated and they remain on plan for further information sharing in the future.

A New Design

CriMNet wasn't so much about passing new laws as it was an effort to realign existing efforts, manage information, and link them through technologies and practices similar to those Target uses to track its inventory. It wasn't new thinking in and of itself, but existing thinking applied to a new situation. All Minnesotans owe Charlie, Jane, and Rich a debt of gratitude for the political courage that it took to do something that innovative.

The CriMNet experience also taught me that common-good outcomes aren't the product of laws alone. The common good is a matter of creating a mix of technologies, institutional cooperation, and people who are willing to lead with new ways of thinking about our communities' challenges. Over the years, my work at Target focused more and more on how to create public policy outcomes outside of the venue of a capitol and the production of legislation. Target continued to work on public safety issues, but our focus quickly blossomed into other types of opportunities where we found just by combining the right types of institutions and like-minded partners, our communities could work together much more productively than if we met solely in a legislative setting.

After nearly eighteen years at Target, I left what was a dream job to pursue another dream: a distinctive civic affairs practice. It had always been to my good fortune to be associated with Target, and my good fortune has been augmented greatly by having my corporate family join me along this path: Target remains an important and cherished part of my work. It's a great outfit.

I've spent over twenty-five years at the intersection of big business, government, politics, media, public safety, philanthropy, academia, and non-governmental organizations. In that time, I've made some wonderful friends, and I've learned a lot about a variety of sectors. The people I've met are usually really good people, but too often their results don't honor the good that they intend. And what I've learned most is that the challenges facing our communities are too complex for any one sector to do much on their own. These challenges require the efforts of many contributors focused on those things that we agree upon and the joint actions that move us forward. It takes a community coming together — not by accident, but by design.

 The challenges facing our communities are too complex for any one sector to do much on their own.

A New Approach

I believe that it is time to change our thinking. And once we change our thinking, we can change the way we interact and produce designs that, not only serve ourselves individually, but serve the common good, too. In fact, as I'll show you, we've been remarkably successful in doing that in the past. If we can look beyond the distracting political heat, we are actually doing quite a nice job of creating common good outcomes in a number of very important arenas. So many of the ways for creating better outcomes are right at our fingertips. Yes, our politics are angry and it seems as if "our voices" aren't being heard in Congress and our state capitols. But, again, what if I told you that part of the problem lies in where we are focusing our attention?

In this book, you'll learn about **Angertainers and the Outrage Industry** and how and why we're being distracted from focusing on what is truly important. You'll learn about **the Naked Eight**, those community imperatives that we almost *never* argue about. You'll learn about an **entire toolbox** of assets that we have — assets that go beyond the tools of laws and politics. You'll see how we've employed that broad variety of tools by creating **habitat designs** that truly honor the common good that respect values and produce economic value at the same time. And finally, you'll learn how you can easily support those designs in your everyday life in ways that enrich you and your community through the **Seven C's of conspicuous common-good consumption.**

Why is all this important? Because, **ultimately, no one does well in a bad community.** It's really expensive to live in a bad community, whether you run a business, a government, or a nonprofit, or belong to a church, mosque, or synagogue. We pay for things that don't enrich our lives, like overcrowded prisons; and we pay for the lost opportunities of directing our resources in better ways, like innovating our schools. We lose good people along the way, and we pay for it in our feelings of despair and helplessness. Frankly, I'm tired of being surrounded by that kind of narrative, and I've met way too many people who feel the same way. So, let's change that!

 Ultimately, no one does well in a bad community.

In *Naked Civics*, you'll learn that if you can tear yourself away from angry politics and the blogs, tweets, political ads, and Sunday-morning talk shows, you'll discover a world that is reinventing itself everyday. It is a world that doesn't lean hard to the political left or right. Rather, it designs and builds confidently in the most important direction of all: forward. This is a very cool story, and one that is already well underway. Indeed, it's always been there. We just need to rediscover it, appreciate it, and use that as the framework for creating better communities. And I promise, it's a story that won't make you angry. In fact, it just might make you smile. And wouldn't that be nice for a change?

A Word on Words

I like words. A lot. They are the tools of a storyteller, and this book is an attempt to begin the journey of telling ourselves a different story than one that we're currently selling ourselves. A word is nothing more than a captured idea. When we agree that when we put the three letters, "d" and "o" and "g" together like this, "dog," it means something to us. When we put them this way — "god" — it means something else. Scattered throughout the book, I've included a number of word constructions that are meant to give more than one meaning — a bit of a pause to ponder some ideas. Why do that? Because this book isn't offering a prescription but permission — permission to start pondering and thinking in ways that we usually don't.

The vast majority of my professional experiences in this arena have occurred within the United States. So, please forgive me for utilizing my country as the canvas for this book. On one hand, it's hardly the case that the U.S. is the only nation suffering from the situation I've described. On the other, as an avid and consistent international traveler and consumer of news throughout the world, I'm confident that much of what you'll read applies beyond the borders of the United States of America. But it is here where I've planted my thinking and quite frankly, I don't feel as versed as I should be in order to comment with confidence on matters outside of my homeland. Those of you reading this elsewhere surely will have that ability, and I welcome your comments and feedback.

As a work intended as a framework for understanding, a good portion of this book will build the case in theory. But as should be true for all impactful thinking, I can't leave you with just some thoughts, especially because for me this hasn't been theory: It's been my practice. So, as you get further into the book, I'll start describing some of my past examples. As you'd imagine, they're not there to show you exactly how you're going to become a designer alongside me, but to demonstrate how I tackled some of these challenges as well as some of the incredible people I've had the pleasure of partnering with.

Let's Get Designing!

This book doesn't purport to have all the answers to all of our societal ills. It's aimed at giving us a perspective, so that we can ask more intelligent questions. Why can't we:

> **Gather** *differently in order to*
> **Think** *differently in order to*
> **Design** *differently in order to*
> **Buy** *differently so we can*
> **Prosper** *together?*

We live in amazing times. Yes, our challenges are great. But we've never had so many different ways to address them. It's time to stop warring over our politics. It's time to strip ourselves down to the essential elements of what we all agree is important and start designing from there. *Naked Civics* isn't just outside-the-box thinking. It's deny-the-box-is-there thinking.

Sudden Illumination Syndrome

YOU KNOW THAT SENSATION WE'VE all experienced these past few years — the one that blinds us with its speed, dishevels our thinking about what we thought we knew, and fills us with daily angst? It's as though the lights had suddenly been flicked on in a dark room. We can see, but we can't focus. I call it Sudden Illumination Syndrome.

Actually, it's been happening for years, as a building tsunami of digital media has engulfed our lives. But in the past few years, Sudden Illumination Syndrome has intensified. Think of it: All that content, those millions and millions of data points — not just from network TV, newspapers, and magazines, but millions upon millions of blogs, websites, tweets, Facebook, Wikipedia, YouTube, cable television, and talk radio. All this has become very familiar to us. Yet, paradoxically, it's also strange and confusing. All this illumination, rather than enlightening us, has thrown us off balance. We're awfully confused right now.

Digital technology has truly brought us into the age of mass multimodal media. Today, it's not just CNN, NBC, FOX, and NPR — we have become part of the media as we tweet, Facebook, Google+, and email each other. And this media is powerful with a capital "P." When you pass something on to someone you know, it oftentimes has more authenticity than you would assign to your local newspaper. And let's face it honestly; too much of our news is nothing more than entertainment dressed up in a news suit. We're awfully cynical right now.

And here's another thing about media these days: Even though we have more access to more information than ever before, mostly we access more information that we already agree with. Combine that self-reinforcing media with decreasing physical interactions with people who think differently from us, and we come up with a heady stew of anonymous anger. It is not only easy to say, "What a stupid idea," but it is comically easy to say, "What an idiot with a stupid idea!" These are things few of us would say to someone face to face — and today we don't have to, except, of course, if you're into those heated protests where people on different sides of an issue seem to enjoy egging each other on, shouting, and jabbing with their fingers. For too many of us, the instant gratification of rage provides a kind of rush or high, a sensation of superiority to a world that we in fact are alienated from. We're awfully coarse right now.

Tied to that is a climate of overreaction that blurs the context and the truth of a situation. For example, Amber Alerts, however useful they may be in some abduction cases, (and indeed there have been wonderful outcomes because of it), have also given many of us a feeling that abductions of children by strangers are more common than they actually are. That feeling turns into action as we plan more and more play dates for our children, instead of letting our kids run around and explore their world, even as we lament that that kind of freedom was what we enjoyed when "We were their age." In fact, my friends in law enforcement tell me that the rate of abductions is about where it's always been for the past fifty years or so, and that in the vast majority of cases, it is an estranged parent who's responsible for the abduction. It doesn't matter because our uncritical awareness has convinced us that our kids are in immediate danger. What is rare has begun to seem common in this suddenly-illuminated world of ours. We're awfully paranoid right now.

Sudden Illumination Syndrome also has exposed us to conspiracy theories that once were considered fringe phenomena. What used to be relegated to the pages of a tabloid is now considered legitimate news: The "birthers" and "truthers" are two of the best known, perhaps too well known. Nearly everyone has a megaphone in the land of Sudden Illumination, and it seems that everyone has his or her volume control knob set to *loud*. We're awfully suspicious right now.

In short, Sudden Illumination Syndrome may throw out a lot of light, but in this case, the light is generating too much heat, too much anxiety, too much anger, and too much ill will. We feel that not only toward one another, we just don't have much trust in any institutions whether they are our governments, our businesses, our schools, our hospitals, political parties, religions, or what is called in some circles "traditional" or "mainstream" media.

All this makes it sound as though Sudden Illumination Syndrome is a bad thing, doesn't it? But in fact, we all know it also has had real benefits. For one thing, if you care to, we now have the ability to easily access more than one or two sources of information — something to which we were limited in a more centralized media age. But we have to take that step outside the gated compounds of our minds if we are to make sense of our new supercharged awareness.

We have to make a shift:

Conte(n)t → Conte(x)t

We have a hyper-abundance of the former, but we need to balance it with much more of the latter. Context is what makes sense of what Sudden Illumination Syndrome has illuminated. Without the deeper connections of context, content is simply entertainment or distraction. Content and distraction are words that reflect the fact that as citizens, we have let ourselves become spectators, cheering on our side and booing the opponents. Too many of us are looking at our communities and our governments — through screens, whether of our televisions, our smartphones, or our laptops.

So here's another shift that we need to make:

Spectator → Actor

Digital media has allowed us to talk like never before. But we aren't putting the same energy into listening. And that means, to me, thinking outside of ourselves and the groups we "identify" with. Simply talking — or shouting! — isn't the same as real interconnection. Put another way: We have lost a sense of civility and the ability to actually deliberate issues. We don't share ideas; instead, we defend our positions and tear the other side down. We don't stop at questioning our opponents' intelligence; it doesn't seem to count unless we question their motives as well.

Even as the problems and challenges we face become larger and more complex, we're finding it harder and harder to come together to face them. And thus, I'll put it out there as such: Our first challenge facing us is *how* we face our challenges. If we don't get better at that, there's not much hope that we'll get much done, either.

 We don't stop at questioning our opponents' intelligence; it doesn't seem to count unless we question their motives as well.

That's one of the main points of this book. Sudden Illumination Syndrome has allowed polarization to dominate the way our communities and country function — or is malfunctioning, really. But here's the thing: *It doesn't have to be that way.* I profoundly believe that the vast majority of us don't wish to live in such a toxically-polarized society. Rather than the current environment of cynicism and despair, we could actually live in happier and more prosperous communities and hand off a better world for our children and theirs. This is not merely wishful thinking. It's been my practice, and for quite a few years, it's been my experience. And it can be your experience, too.

If we are to get beyond the destructive fear and distrust that Sudden Illumination Syndrome has engendered, we need to get re-centered, rather than being pulled to the left or right, and we certainly need to get past the idea that "our side" has the market cornered on good ideas, good people, and good intentions.

One other key point I'll be making in *Naked Civics* is: Our current challenges didn't happen by accident. They are a product of our civic *designs*. The word "design" may make most of us think of endeavors like graphics and architecture. But design is really about the creation and use of tools. And as you'll read, what we design aesthetically and digitally is just a part of what we can do as designers. We also can (re)design our communities.

The problem with many of our current civic designs is that they no longer work the way they were originally intended. We certainly can see that in our political system, where perpetuating conflict has become more important than actually making progress on the challenges we must confront.

But here's the great thing: *Anything that has been designed can be redesigned.* Redesigning doesn't always have to be as hard as pushing a law through Congress. But it does mean that more of us will have to get back to the idea of being citizens who are active in building a better community. That's not to say that it will always be easy, but it will probably be easier than you initially imagine. And it will be fulfilling — certainly more fulfilling than the toxicity that we currently breathe every day.

To be successful in this endeavor, we have to reclaim a great many things. One of them is the word *civics*. It sounds like an old-fashioned term, redolent of long afternoons in a public school classroom, tuning out a teacher droning on about the term lengths of elected officials. Enough of that! I'm taking the word back because it is a rich one. Civics is about how we live together, and how our lives interconnect. And it concerns active involvement and listening, rather than shaking our fists at phones, computer screens, and flatscreen TVs. Civics also requires *civility*, which means taking a deep breath before we react to a news item or Twitter post in order to think out our beliefs — and to see whether we have good reasons to believe them. Civics also requires that rather than cheer, boo, and otherwise grandstand, we actually empathize even with people who we "know" are "wrong." So, toss out that picture of a boring classroom and replace it with ones that have kids running around your street playing tag, rocking concerts, vibrant downtowns, and lush parks full of greenery and peace, and what it takes to produce it all. That's what the word civics means to me.

 Civics is about how we live together, and how our lives interconnect.

And as we shift our definition of that cherished word, I believe that it would serve us well to strip naked — that is, to remove our most cherished prejudices, perceptions, and stereotypes about politics, public policy, and other people and other "groups."

This will require, among other things, that we become aware of the strengths and limitations of our civic tools. I'll talk more about what I mean by tools later in this book. But for now, here's a useful way to think of them: At their core, tools are the inventions that we create in the attempt to put some order around our ever-changing world. Our tools have enormous power, and history shows that we're incredibly able to create new ones when we need to. What we need now are redesigned tools.

The toolbox for building the public good includes what you traditionally think of: government, laws, and regulations. We'll always need these — I'm certainly not saying that we can or should do away with government or politics. Quite the contrary. But we do need other tools as well. And one of our main challenges currently is that we're not very used to thinking of anything but government, laws, and regulations when it comes to producing the common good. That's not only a limiting way for us to think, but it puts us squarely back into the angry environment of our current political landscape. Folks, it's not the **only** place to have conversations about how we live and thrive next to each other. Seriously.

 Tools are the inventions that we create in the attempt to put some order around our ever-changing world.

One final point: I don't want to suggest that *Naked Civics* is a recipe book for a perfect world. Such a world can never exist. We'll never all think the same way — and despite the polarization that Sudden Illumination Syndrome has caused, that's actually a good thing. Disagreeing is incredibly important. Being disagreeable is another thing, and something that we could stand less of. This book doesn't have all the answers. It's intended to stimulate a conversation about public life — one that leads to different actions. Yes, I hope you'll find what I say is worth listening to. As I mentioned in the introduction, I've worked in a great number of sectors and worked with a great variety of leaders over the past couple dozen years. And here's the thing I've learned over and over: The person who really doesn't care about our communities doing better is extremely rare. Almost all of us want a fairly similar outcome. But we're just stymied. We all have much more power to make our communities better than we've been led to believe. We'll get to that "led to believe" in a bit. It's an important challenge that we need to address.

So, let's begin the adventure. Let's be civil. Let's listen to each other. Let's learn from each other. Let's start interacting differently. And let's start rebuilding a common-good world where we all can flourish.

As a first step, let's look at one design that has driven us from common ground. I call it the Outrage Industry.

That's Angertainment!

SUDDEN ILLUMINATION SYNDROME has given rise to — and is perpetuated by — a highly profitable Angertainment business. The stars in the Angertainment universe are names more familiar to many of us than those of our legislative representatives. Glenn Beck, Bill Maher, Rush Limbaugh, Keith Olbermann, Ann Coulter, Bill O'Reilly, Rachel Maddow, and innumerable other performers nationally and locally are starring today and tonight in yet another production of *The Merchants of Venom*. They're making big money in what I call the Outrage Industry, stoking the steam engines of our worries and anger. They feed off fear, and they also use it to manufacture more of it.

The Outrage Industry plays out on the stage of advocacy and lobbying organizations, the number of which has exploded in the past number of years. (See the chart at the end of this chapter.)

By and large, these organizations advocate not for the common good, but for the *insular* good — namely, what's good solely for the interests that they represent. Don't get me wrong: That's what they do by design. For the most part, they don't advertise that they're working for the betterment of the common good, although too often they are successful in portraying their particular interest as pivotal and singular toward all that is good and supportable. Name any cause or interest, and there's likely to be an organization (often several) that is battling for it in the halls of government, online, or in mailboxes. Organizations, some of which have a staff consisting of one highly caffeinated individual, advocate on behalf of governments, businesses, labor, churches, and other nonprofit interests. Whether you are a pauper or a billionaire, there is someone "representing" your interests. The plain fact is that these days, *everybody* is part of a special interest.

Within the advocacy space, there are spectrums of representation on every issue. In the environmental movement, for example, you have everything from the Nature Conservancy, which buys and preserves green spaces on the private market, to the Earth Liberation Front, which likes to blow up things now and then (and which the FBI has listed as a terrorist group). But in politics, we too conveniently refer to these issues in monolithic terms. Here's the environmental lobby and here's the labor lobby and here's the business lobby. Though if you look more closely, there are often dramatic differences between groups within these issue sets. For instance, the trade unions don't always have the same political agenda as government employee unions. In other words, although every issue seems prone to being over politicized and infused with anger, not every advocacy group or advocate is playing the outrage game. But more often than not, we lump them all together and pit them against each other. It's a shame, because advocacy in and of itself is an important part of how we address complex issues as a society.

(out)rage

The chart at the end of this chapter lists the number of advocates who have *formally* registered. There probably are innumerable informal advocates as well. The upshot is that we have an environment with a lot of mouthpieces out there. As Robert D. Putnam notes in his 1995 book, *Bowling Alone*, unlike service organizations, like the Elks and Moose, few of these advocacy organizations have meetings of their memberships. The fact that these old-line community service organizations are shrinking in membership speaks to the increasing disconnect between organization and membership. "Joining" an advocacy organization is mostly a matter of writing a check and hitting the send button. Once that's done, your voice becomes that of the organization.

The political parties themselves seem to be some of the biggest stage actors in the Outrage Industry. Perhaps it is because so many of our current challenges lie outside of the capacity of our political structures alone. Commensurate with the inability of Democrats or Republicans being able to actually make significant headway, they revert instead to scaring the public about the other side: "Forget about voting for me — what you need to do is vote against THEM!" It really is quite perverse in some ways: The parties are increasingly comprised with some of the most strident angry voices. Yet, according to field research done for the centrist political movement No Labels (mentioned later), independent voters are a very large and growing part of our electorate.

It's important to realize that the organizations that make up the Outrage Industry are skillful marketers. But you already knew that, didn't you? They know what emotional buttons to press, and how to press them for maximum effect. They rely upon the instantaneous, knee-jerk responses of their constituencies. And they gather those responses to put pressure on elected officials. You probably know the script better than you think: "Government run amok," "Corporate jet owners and other fat cats," "People who don't live according to traditional family values." etc. Blurted out in TV sound bites or embedded in fundraising letters, these are the buzzwords coming from both political sides.

Many of the players in the Outrage Industry focus on a single issue, whether it's abortion, global warming, gun control, or what have you. That single-mindedness is key: The Outrage Industry wants us to look at things in a binary way. They (and those who support them) are number one; the "other side" is a big zero. To more and more of these groups, "the other side" is the enemy that they must fight with everything they have. *We can't let them win. They want to destroy everything we hold dear. And we can never question our own side.*

There's something else about many Outrage Industry organizations: While they generate a lot of sound and fury about problems, they don't want to actually solve those problems. Too often, these interests are actually solution-adverse. The reason is simple: If the problem or issue that an advocacy organization has trumpeted is "solved," then it's likely that it is no longer needed. Whether it's the U.S. Chamber of Commerce, the AFL-CIO, or the Sierra Club, too many advocacy operations can't afford to let you know there's actually progress being made on an issue. Why? Because when there's progress, that's when they start feeling vulnerable and that their membership (and income) is going to dry up. So, they must keep shouting, they must keep inciting fear and anger, and they must keep raising more funds — all checks, but not much balance.

And just as you know that these interests are skillful marketers, I bet you'll recognize that there's a number of tried-and-true tactics that they usually revert to. One is: Leave the middle ground undefined. The abortion debate is a lot like that. If you poll Americans, consistently you'll find that most are pro-choice. But they're not just pro-choice. They get nervous about preventing an abortion in the case of rape, but they also get very nervous about allowing the procedure in the third trimester. It's a highly complex issue. Yet, you'll never hear the pro-life crowd or the pro-choice crowd define it around that middle ground. That's not where the political action is. It's not where the money is, either, by the way.

 Too often, these interests are actually solution-adverse. The reason is simple: If the problem or issue that an advocacy organization has trumpeted is "solved," then it's likely that it is no longer needed.

Then, there's the old slippery slope. You know: First they'll take away my armor-piercing bullets — and pretty soon, they'll be taking away my handguns and my ability to defend myself against an increasingly socialist government. Or: Once abortion is "acceptable," the next step is euthanasia of the sick, elderly, and severely handicapped. Or: Once they drill here, they'll drill everywhere.

There's also the strategy where you characterize every sector by its worst actors — as its caricatures. This is where every CEO is a rapacious money grabber, every priest is a pedophile, every politician is on the take, every lobbyist is illegally throwing money under the table for influence, every union member is lazy and greedy, and every environmental activist is economically clueless. Of course, we know these "facts" aren't true, but it sure is a convenient way of defining entire sectors, so you can vilify them before you oppose them. And let's not kid ourselves. These worst actors sure do make for entertaining news fodder, right?

These tactics are age-old and they all have one goal: Thwart compromise. This is war, folks. There is no surrender. We must support our troops. If we cede just a little bit of ground, the American way of life (or our freedom, or the ideals that made this country great, or our prosperity, our natural environment, or whatever) will slide irrevocably down the mountain of moral and economic decline.

I just noted the binary worldview of the Outrage Industry. Maybe that's why it has been so successful in digital communication,

(d)anger

particularly the Internet. The World Wide Web makes it very easy to gather more eyeballs, more mouthpieces, and more money. And it's incredibly easy to provide more content of discontent through blogs, videos, and other forms of Angertainment to whip up fear and distraction.

When we narrow the possibilities of where we do our thinking, we narrow the possibilities of how we think.

But the Outrage Industry wouldn't be so successful if it weren't for the way our political system has been designed and more so how it is being currently used and abused. We seem bent on thinking of every societal issue as a matter of laws and politics and not much more. And when we narrow the possibilities of where we do our thinking, we narrow the possibilities of how we think. And we also narrow our capacity for possibilities beyond the purely political realm. It's a damn shame, because underlying all this mess, our legislative bodies are constructed using a brilliant design.

To be sure, our legislative system is purpose-built for conflict. There are committee hearings, there is party identification, and there is issue identification. It's not a bad design for discussing policy, if there's truly a discussion about policy: Where you're black and I'm white, over time, with enough give and take, we get to gray. But we have so overemphasized the politics of every issue that the adversarial design has transformed our capitol buildings into temples of conflict. Far too often, the conversations aren't about policy; they're about politics. In this scenario, black is black and white is white, and we both get killed for going gray. If you put every issue into an environment that is purpose-built for adversarialism, then you will get an adversarial view of the issue and the participants will act ... as adversaries. In some ways, it's as simple as that. Pay people by the fight and guess what you get, right?

Congress, of course, is the main soundstage for the production of Fear Compromise by the Outrage Industry and the Angertainers. It is a true but unfortunate state of affairs these days that staying in office requires endless money-raising. And the Outrage Industry has some of the deepest pockets. Congressional representatives go home every weekend and meet with interest groups. They have town halls where they hear angry people, they meet with industry groups, and they meet with labor groups. But too often, they're not speaking with people who have a broader sense of the common good. They're listening to and getting money from advocates for the insular good. Don't get me wrong: It's not that our elected representatives don't thirst for meeting with average folks. But it's getting awfully difficult to do so. And like so many other instances I'll mention in this book, what I'm getting at is that this is yet another case of generally really good people being forced into less than stellar behavior because of bigger design issues.

Elected officials didn't always operate in this kind of bubble. Years ago, before the dominance of the Outrage Industry, before the easy mobility of jumping on a jet to cross the nation, before the housing prices in Washington, DC went through the roof, the two sides actually hung out with each other. They'd get together with their colleagues, have a cocktail, talk about each other's spouses and kids — who usually went to school together. It wasn't until fairly recently that elected officials went home every weekend. But that was before "not being in touch with their district" became a huge political threat. These days, members can't socialize with each other because they have a flight home to catch. They battle each other at the factory, and as soon as the whistle blows, they leave the premises, they go home, and they generally aren't meeting with people of opposing viewpoints. Instead, they're forced into raising money — and reinforcing their side. They simply have to do that — not just to get reelected, but also to obtain choice professional promotions. Those who can raise the most money get the best committee assignments, and they're the ones who get selected to chair the most powerful committees, giving them the best ability to raise more money.

Meanwhile, the ideals and ideas of the common good, the kinds of efforts that truly require complex understanding and compromise, are rarely addressed, except through lip service. If you're not outraged, you're not getting attention.

The Citizen as Spectator

So how did this design come to be? Why has the number of these organizations grown so large, and why have they become so dominant in our policy discussions? Mostly, it's because we the people have let all this happen. Don't kid yourself. It's not as easy as blaming one party or one special interest.

During the past forty years, we have increasingly sequestered ourselves in insular intellectual compounds. In essence, we have outsourced most of our involvement in the public realm to organizations. It started in the 1930s, when government became much larger and more activist. And while the New Deal brought about a great many public benefits, it also came with significant costs, beyond the fiscal realities of entitlements. We started on a path of creating tax-supported government programs to take care of each other, rather than relying on other community institutions. As we'll talk about later, tools like these programs have power — not just good or bad, but usually both.

We can also see this civic outsourcing as a logical outcome of our post-World War II prosperity. After the war, we began to move out of the cities, where different "classes" jostled shoulder to shoulder, to cleaner, more spacious suburban realms. And whether we were workers enjoying the benefits of strong union contracts and low unemployment or the new professional class created largely by

GI Bill-financed college degrees, we could increasingly afford to outsource civic involvement. We had money in our wallets.

To be sure, the members of this expanding middle class were great joiners in the 1950s and early 1960s — churches and synagogues were full, Kiwanis and Jaycees chapters flourished, and people knocked on doors for their favored candidates. But the postwar era also saw the rise of television and the boom in mass marketing, which fueled a focus on consumption. As the Cato Institute's Brink Lindsey notes in his 2007 book, *The Age of Abundance*, that astonishing prosperity "liberated" us from the various communities — religious institutions, labor unions, fraternal and charitable organizations, and the commercial and residential neighborhoods where we grew up — that had helped us get by during difficult financial times. By the 1960s, these were communities that many of us had found restrictive. We began to shift our sense that happiness came from activity in the public realm (as Aristotle was one of the first to argue) and relocated it to our "personal lives" conducted in private.

But that consumerist isolation wouldn't have taken root without the changes in the political realm that began in the late 1960s. The traumas and upheavals of that era are familiar, and we don't need to re-recount them in detail here. But to provide more context for the rise of our modern-day Outrage Industry, I'd like to make a few points.

The first is that the main political parties themselves became more insular and monocultural. Up through the early 1960s, the Democratic and Republican parties accommodated, often uneasily, members of different political persuasions. Moderate and liberal Republicans were common, as were conservative Southern and urban-ethnic Democrats. After signing the Civil Rights Act of 1964, President Lyndon Johnson told an aide, "We have *lost the South* for a generation." He was referring to the Democratic Party; two generations later, Southern Democrats certainly haven't disappeared, but there are far fewer now. The 1972 nomination of George McGovern was the point of no return for most conservative Democrats. Meanwhile, with Ronald Reagan as their standard bearer, well-organized and well-financed social conservative Republicans were beginning their long march to dominate the GOP.

In short, the parties no longer allow uneasy but useful coalitions that reach across the aisle from time to time. To borrow a term from mass marketing, parties have become *brands*. These days, the parties are national brands reflecting a national strategy. And their leaders insist that their members stay on message. The Speaker of the U.S. House in the 1970s and 1980s, Thomas "Tip" O'Neill, once famously declared, "All politics is local." That's less true today. National party organizations dispense much of the funding local candidates need; and if those candidates don't toe the national line, they can find themselves short of funds — or facing a well-financed primary opponent. And that's just the money that's coming from the parties. Usually, that pot of money is dwarfed by what comes in from outside interests aiming at swaying voters.

Meanwhile, electoral districts have become more and more politically homogenous. Bill Bishop's 2009 book, *The Big Sort*, detailed how Americans are increasingly able to move away from each other thanks to cheap oil and what was a booming housing industry. It discusses how we divided ourselves into communities that are often physically gated — and, even more likely, philosophically gated. It's pretty well assumed these days that if you're living in an urban core, you're in Blue country. If you're living out in the exurbs — those areas beyond the first- and second-ring suburbs — your political stripes usually run Red.

Techno-utopians once argued that the Internet would break down barriers like these. The digital multiverse would open us up to viewpoints and cultures beyond the narrow-cast lenses of non-digital media. For some of us, it has. But it also has the capability of narrowing our frames of reference. In his new book, *The Filter Bubble: What the Internet Is Hiding from You*, former MoveOn.org Executive Director Eli Pariser, who guided that liberal organization's evolution into an online powerhouse, notes that Facebook, Google, and other Internet portals and hubs have designed algorithms that are "personalizing" the Internet. As Pariser told CNN.com in May 2011, "A couple of years ago, when you Googled something, everyone would get the same result. Now, when I've done these experiments, you can really get these dramatically different results. One person Googles and sees a lot of news about protests and the other person gets travel agents talking about traveling to Egypt."

In other words, despite the power of Sudden Illumination Syndrome, Google and the others are aiding us in our desire to limit our exposure to items beyond our focus. Politically, this means that we don't access information aimed at "the other side." When I access information that I already agree with, it just might not be the same information that you're accessing and agree with. The voices we access encourage us to perceive of people who don't think like "us" as a threat. "They want to allow people to carry guns anywhere in public!" vs. "They want to take away my Constitutional right to bear arms!" "They want to continue to throw money at failing schools!" vs. "They want to gut the public schools that made our country great!" "They are anti-life!" vs. "They want to control women's bodies!" And of course, this becomes most worrisome when these voices are wielded with righteous fervor. Watch out for the fervor, folks.

Ultimately, perhaps, the Outrage Industry has succeeded so well, and has kept fear of "the other side" alive, because of our great anxiety over *loss*. In many cases, we are afraid that if the other side succeeds, we'll lose what prosperity we have. (That's a reason "socialism" remains such a powerful scare word among some groups.) Business organizations want to maintain their wealth; senior citizens' groups worry about protecting their entitlements. Again, this shouldn't be surprising when you consider the environment that we conduct these debates: Adversaries naturally see contests as zero sum — if you gain, I lose.

But in other cases, the loss certain groups are battling to defend is a loss of self-identity. In *Years of Hope, Days of Rage*, his 1993 book on the rise and decline of 1960s political activism, Todd Gitlin used the term "expressive politics" to describe how many people have tightly interwoven their political beliefs with their sense of self. Forty years ago, you would have seen signs and bumper stickers during a teacher's strike saying, "Support Our Teachers." Now, those signs are more likely to say, "*I* Support Teachers." The first is seeking to engage other people; the second is an expression of personal identity. To compromise means to sacrifice a kind of authenticity, a sense of purity — and to compromise suggests that you aren't fully committed to your values.

Indeed, these days, compromise means losing my membership, my identity, and my vote. And to question my side's positions means losing face. And why should an advocacy group let its guard down and make the first move to compromise when it's not too likely that the other side will let *its* guard down? For a conservative Republican to even suggest a tax increase on wealthy Americans would mean being pilloried by Outrage Industrialists, such as the Club for Growth, for veering from the proper ideological dogma. And it is equally difficult for liberal Democrats to seriously reform governmental programs when they are being threatened by their own Outrage Industry versions in the form of public-employee unions and other interests.

If you're looking as to why advocacy is a booming growth industry, it is worth noting that one reason is that no longer is it solely

intolerant

focused on traditional political structures and the political calendar. Advocates lobby within the calendar of the legislative bodies, but they also lobby through the media and they lobby through the boardroom where there is no set calendar. The battle is ongoing — the campaign never ends. We see increased use of boycotts and the rise of various ThisBusinessSucks.com sites. Both professional and amateur advocates react instantly to the news cycle, keeping us on edge at every moment. There just isn't an advocacy season anymore. The geography may have expanded, but we're bringing the same "us versus them" mind-set with us wherever we travel.

Advocacy Goes BOOM!

There is a lot of money in advocacy — and a lot of advocates chasing it. The data below are from the Senate Office of Public Records. As you can see, the numbers have steadily increased every year, with the exception of 2001. Interestingly, the number of lobbyists has decreased in the last three years (a result of the recession, perhaps?), but the amount of money spent has not decreased. Fewer companies are spending just as much money on their lobbying efforts. Most sources attribute the long-term growth of lobbyists to the increased scope of the government and specific issues. For example, when Congress deliberates on energy legislation, the number of lobbying groups for this issue also grows. Sources also agree that the number of lobbyists began to grow in the 1980s. Although hard numbers aren't available, one source estimates that the number of lobbyists doubled in the years 1981 to 2006. The study based its estimate on the number of "domestic corporate lobbying presence" listed in the *Washington Representatives Directory*, which increased from 4,256 to 7,794.

Number of Lobbyists		Total Lobbying Spending
1998	10,404	$1.44 billion
1999	12,943	$1.44 billion
2000	12,542	$1.56 billion
2001	11,845	$1.64 billion
2002	12,128	$1.82 billion
2003	12,924	$2.04 billion
2004	13,166	$2.17 billion
2005	14,075	$2.43 billion
2006	14,531	$2.62 billion
2007	14,885	$2.85 billion
2008	14,212	$3.30 billion
2009	13,721	$3.49 billion
2010	12,986	$3.49 billion

Numbers for the increase of non-government organizations (NGOs) are harder to find, especially since defining them is difficult (neighborhood organizations can be considered NGOs, for instance). For those of you who may not be familiar with that term, an NGO is simply an organization, more often than not supported by member donations, that involves itself in certain public arenas. Examples are the Red Cross, the Sierra Club, and Doctors Without Borders. There are thousands and thousands of them.

And all the sources I've looked at agree that the number of NGOs has dramatically increased since the 1980s. The World Association of Non-Governmental Agencies lists 21,619 international NGOs in the United States. Domestically, the numbers of groups considered NGOs have been estimated anywhere between one million and two million! Not that long ago (December 1999), *The Economist* reported that of the one million NGOs in the U.S., 70 percent of them were younger than thirty years.

But at that, there are many categories of NGOs where it is hard to get any hard numbers at all.

And who do you think is the biggest advocate on the block? It may surprise you, but it's our governments themselves. As with every other sector, the public sector's lobbying efforts have skyrocketed. According to the Scripps Howard News Service and the Center for Responsive Politics, we currently have more than twenty-three hundred government and public educational institutions spending more than $1.2 billion advocating their interests in front of Congress. And that doesn't even scratch the surface of what is also being spent at the state level. Could it be that this is one of the biggest drivers of why we tend to throw government solutions at nearly every public challenge?

While the exact numbers are debatable, it is folly to deny that our communities are producing a significant increase in the volume of professional, semiprofessional, and hobbyist advocacy. Again, this is not to argue that advocacy in and of itself is a bad thing because it's not. But let's be honest: This sea of special interests is by and large jockeying for attention, so that their special interest is taken care of — and too often at the expense of the common good.

If I Had a Hammer

Actually, it seems that's *all* people have in politics these days, particularly in how we talk about public policy. Turn on your TV or radio, and chances are you'll run into a campaign ad that says a version of one of two things:

1. "My opponent voted to raise taxes!"
2. "My opponent voted to cut government spending!"

If you were going to remodel your basement, would you grab a hammer and look around and ask, "Okay, what needs hammering?" Probably not. Yet, when it comes to how we service the common good, it seems to come down to how much or how little government we throw at the challenge.

Please don't misconstrue my point: Government's involvement in the common good is critical. But shouldn't we ask ourselves whether there are any other tools in the toolbox? Wouldn't it be nice if you could hear a campaign ad that went something like this?

"My opponent failed to be creative — failed to bring the taxpayers more value by intelligently combining the services of government with the energies of other sectors working in combination as they all more successfully met our needs."

Our challenges are many, they are difficult, and they are complex. Why would we want to limit ourselves to just one tool — namely, politics?

The Political Design Behind
Our Political System

WHEN YOU HEAR THE TERM "design," you likely think of things like logos, Photoshop, and well-oiled machines. What you likely do *not* think of is government. But, whether it's good or bad, our government is a design. We know the blueprint of our government as the Constitution and Bill of Rights, of course. And lately, it would seem that, like so many other institutions in our country, our government is failing us. But what if it isn't the design of government, but rather the design of our politics that is to blame? We're not used to thinking of politics as separate and apart from our governmental institutions, but separating the two just may lead to a better ability to redesign and make what's wrong, right, while not messing with what's actually working.

It's worth noting that in over two centuries since our Constitution was enacted, we've never ever failed to install a government. We've never had a violent revolution break out because of an election outcome (not counting the Civil War, which one could argue was set in motion regardless of Lincoln's election or not). Now that's quite some feat, and it points to the fact that not *everything* is broken.

But *some* things are most definitely broken and much of it is due to the fact that we allow our political institutions to set up and operate our governmental designs in such a way that it allows political aims to trump all and leaves hardly any space for actual legislating. It seems a strange and unfortunate anomaly that in a country where you can find numerous makes and models of cars, where you can design your morning coffee in dozens and dozens of ways, where you can find your particular style in just about every other aspect of your life, we allow small bands of political activists to severely limit our choices when it comes to who is crafting the nation's laws. Think about that. How many calling plan options do you currently have for your phone? Want to see a movie tonight? How many movies can you choose from? Go to your local grocery store. How many kinds of milk are in the dairy case? Yet, when it comes to our political choices, we are most often left with just two very strong and competing flavors from which to choose.

On Election Day, we're presented with extremely limited and extremely drawn options that are chosen for us by a comically tiny sliver of hyper-partisan citizens called the party faithful. Their faith and their pledges are to their party, not the country. Not very representative is it? And again, the current model for government *at its core* isn't a bad design. What has happened is that we've created a very powerful political design that dominates and is allowed to pervert the underlying genius of a government by the people, for the people, and based on a balance of powers. Rather than focusing on the future of the United States, we have allowed an environment where our leaders are rewarded by their dogged focus on one party's dominance over the other.

 It seems a strange and unfortunate anomaly that we allow small bands of political activists to severely limit our choices when it comes to who is crafting the nation's laws.

That's not what the Founding Fathers intended when they designed the American system. Indeed, a quick perusal through history books will show you that they positively warned us against the power of political parties. And while we have purposefully created a design where it is very difficult to change our Constitution, so much of what we could be doing is changing congressional rules, which is a far less complex exercise.

Think of what could happen if we made just this one political design change: The Speaker of the House is the person who receives the majority of votes from members of the House of Representatives, not just the votes of the majority party. It's not hard to see that the consequence of this one change would be that future Speakers would be much more non-partisan in their makeup. Perhaps then, we would have a political body that isn't as fixated on politics.

At this point, I should make a confession. Despite this long litany of criticism, I strongly believe that political parties and advocacy groups are in themselves not bad things. We need them. There isn't an issue worthy of being called an important challenge that isn't also incredibly complex and full of consequence. Politicians have a very difficult job and one that far too few realize as such. And as a core utility, advocates are necessary educators to political decision makers. Indeed, in my years of work in public affairs, the overwhelming majority of the people I know in these circles are good, smart people who *do* care about the common good. I'm serious — they are the kind of people whom you'd want as your next-door neighbor. And they are some of the quickest to bemoan the uncivil state of our political cultures. But despite their good intentions, too often the systems that they work within continue to incent and produce anything but that. They're trapped in a *bad design*, one that has made our civic relationships plain dysfunctional.

The reason so many of these good people in the advocacy business end up acting badly is because we've thrown ourselves together with an insular adversarial mind-set and meet in an adversarial setting. So, what do we get? Adversarialism. Whether it is in a capitol building or in the digital ether, the bulk of us have a mind-set that social ills need to be — and can only be — regulated by laws. Those laws are created in what could be described as a hyper-labeled environment. Exercising our voices isn't bad. It's *where and how* we exercise. That's the issue here. So, in *addition* to the temples of conflict, we should be gathering elsewhere as well. The design of such spaces is something I'll discuss in Chapter 12.

But in order to create these spaces, we must understand, or understand again, that our world moves forward only through compromise. The United States was founded on compromise, between Federalists and Anti-Federalists. Do you think that there might have been a few heated arguments when the representatives of the states came together in Philadelphia during the summer of 1787? But despite some profound differences — about just how democratic the new country should be, for instance — they were able to focus on the fundamental truthfulness of their joint mission and find ways to compromise. It wasn't just wise to do so — it was honorable.

Certainly, we should regret some of the compromises they made — for instance, letting slaves count as three-fifths of a person, while not allowing them even three-fifths of a vote. (Not to mention the fugitive slave clause in Article IV, Section 2.) But the Declaration of Independence did say, "All men are created equal." And by writing that line, Jefferson and the Declaration's other authors placed within this nation's DNA the thinking that would ultimately destroy slavery. What's more, the Founding Fathers of the U.S. Constitution did put in place the tools and institutions that would allow the destruction of that "peculiar institution" to occur, however painful that process was. Those tools and institutions would ultimately help propel the Civil Rights Act of 1964, which wouldn't have happened had Democrats like Southerner Lyndon Johnson and Republicans like Northerner Everett Dirksen not come together to make that a reality.

And those great legislative achievements wouldn't have happened at all if black people hadn't marched — outside of the halls of Congress — and if white people hadn't come to Selma, Birmingham, and Washington, DC, and marched with them. In doing so, we have gone from "I have a dream" to "We have a black president."

In other words, there has always been and continues to be a legitimate place for emotion in our political discourse. You'll get no debate from me: anger is a great motivator. It can bring about big and important changes. But take it too far, feed on it for too long, and watch out: We fall in love with that anger, and we use it to prevent us from seeing "the other side" as a group of human beings whose viewpoints and life experiences are just as valid (if "wrong"!) as our own. Anger does not make a nutritious long-term diet. Another way to look at this is that if we define every little thing in our world as a crisis, it hurts our ability to respond to those situations that actually are a crisis.

So, here's where we find ourselves today as a citizenry, my friends: We think of the common good merely as the product of our laws that we produce. And we produce laws through politics. As I've noted, we move left, we move right, but rarely do we move forward.

 Anger does not make a nutritious long-term diet.

But the vexing truth of it all is this: Most of us *do* want to move forward. Most of us know that the huge challenges our localities and nation face require compromises. We live our lives outside of politics, comfortable (usually) with the thought that, "I can't, indeed shouldn't, get my way on *everything*." The point is that the Outrage Industry, whether it's "left" or "right," liberal or conservative, doesn't speak for us — just some of us, and even then, just part of the time. While the majority of us don't fit easy, mass-market political labeling, we haven't put ourselves in a sufficiently strong position of influence to counteract the sound and fury of the Outrage Industry. So, if we want to be heard, we need to design a way where we can have more influence around the common good.

And that requires us to rebuild a sense of civics, of working to-gether to design *communities* — "community" means common space, and it refers to more than just a geographical location — where the common good can flourish. It's going to take a mind-set that while laws are indeed important, they are not enough. We are going to think of ourselves as bigger than political players and that our society is bigger than the sum total of laws that we pass or kill.

To accomplish that kind of redesign, we will need tools: *All* of our tools — not just the political ones.

Wait a Minute! You Were a Lobbyist, Right?

Indeed and happy to say so. Advocacy is an important activity in our democracy, and I don't agree with those who "want to do away with all lobbyists." This attitude is born out of a perspective that is largely ignorant of what lobbyists do and the actual practice of lobbying. But I can hardly blame folks for that attitude, as they rarely hear about the profession except when there is an egregious jerk defining the entire profession with his or her activities. The fact of the matter is that legislating is hard business ... it's a world filled with complexities, and lobbyists have important specific information that is necessary for good decision-making. Lobbying, when well done, can be very important. But we sure do have a lot of it going on, don't we?

And it's like most everything else in our world — mostly done well, but boy do we hear about it when it's not. That activity is really upsetting. . . especially to the folks who do it right.

Tool Time

SINCE THE TIME WHEN HUMAN beings began to think more broadly about their lives beyond where to get their next meal, we have stared up at the moon and the stars, wondered about all the chaos and ambiguity in the world, and asked, "How do I keep my loved ones safe and well fed?" As we evolved as social beings, we began to ask broader questions: "How do we create a community where everyone feels safe and well fed? And how do we build such a community?"

The answer is tools. Homo sapiens discovered early on that they were inherently great toolmakers; since then, we have built up quite a large toolbox. As we began to utilize that master tool we call agriculture, for instance, we quickly honed and perfected the tools associated with it. We made our stone axes a little sharper. In time, we traded up for bronze tools, and then steel. We went from using hand tools for planting to horse-drawn plows. And today, we have air-conditioned, GPS-located combines that allow one person to plant and harvest large areas of cropland that not long ago would have required the work of hundreds to sow and reap.

When we talk about tools, we usually think of technologies. But some of the most powerful tools the world has ever seen are institutions. We may not think of them as tools, but that's certainly what they are: designs constructed to accomplish social tasks, to bring order from chaos. And like that journey from stone hoes to mechanical combines, our institutions have grown and morphed over time. As we developed the tools to grow more crops than we actually needed, we developed institutions for trade — I could exchange my surplus grain for the woolen or cotton garments you spent all day making. We created a myriad of businesses to create and manage our commercial activities. And to make trade more effective, we started to "silo" our societies: creating specialized jobs beyond hunting and gathering. We created societal structures — governments and religions — that organized our communal lives into efficient order. We created armies to protect our newfound wealth and stability.

 When we talk about tools, we usually think of technologies. But some of the most powerful tools the world has ever seen are institutions.

Without these tools, we'd each live the kind of lives that Thomas Hobbes famously described as "solitary, poor, nasty, brutish, and short." In many ways, institutions are simply coordinated design conversations. We agree that we're going to create a market in which to sell our grain, animals, or handmade products — just like we agree that our money or hours of labor or bartered items are worth such and such an amount on a given day. It works like that in our everyday lives all over the place. Such as: Hey, let's get a bunch of people to go over to that tall building over there from Monday through Friday and try to create a profit for this thing we'll call Widgets R Us.

Like technologies, institutions are inventions — inventions that allow other inventions to flourish. The fact that you're reading this, whether as printed hard copy or on an electronic reader like a Kindle, an iPad, or a Nook, is due to institutions: businesses that harvested the trees or mined the rare earths, companies that designed the device, (whether it's a book or e-reader), along with the manufacturers, marketers, and retailers — not to mention the schools that taught the authors the most effective and (they hope) engaging ways to use that particularly multifaceted tool, the alphabet.

Then, there are the institutions designed to allow those other institutions to function and flourish: laws, regulations, and the governments that oversee them. Whether it's the local school board, a state's election commission, the court system, or the federal Securities and Exchange Commission, institutions interconnect to provide the trust necessary for human beings to generate wealth and ideas.

All of these things were intended and designed: the computer manufacturers, the publishers, the country we live in and the design documents — the Declaration of Independence, the Constitution, and the Bill of Rights — that were its blueprint. But of all of our tools — all of our technologies and all of our institutions — perhaps the most powerful tool of all is how human beings' technologies and institutions all relate to each other. This is called institutional thinking: our mind-sets. It is at once so incredibly a simple concept and yet so very complex in its application: A mind-set is the perspective you bring to how you approach a situation and how you choose to act upon it ... and start employing other tools.

Perhaps the most powerful tool of all is how human beings' technologies and institutions all relate to each other. This is called institutional thinking: our mind-sets.

In the vast majority of households in this country (and in many other countries), we set the fork on the left side of the plate, and the knife and spoon on the right. We put a napkin on our lap and chew with our mouths shut. That's what we consider proper table manners. But what are those? They are simply the way we think about dining together. Table manners are a type of institutional thinking. That's true of nearly any form of social etiquette. True, it's perfectly proper to slurp your noodles in Tokyo, but it would be offensive to do so in Topeka. It's just the way our cultures work — how each of them builds common ground.

It's easy to take our tools for granted — and at the same time, become infatuated with them. So much so, that we can come to believe that, at least over time, they can and will solve all of our problems. Yet, if we are honest with ourselves, we know that it's not that simple. We have been enormously successful in employing tools for the common good. And we have been equally good at using them for disastrous results. A steel mill can produce the pressed metal panels that make up the housing of a washing machine; it can also produce the barrel and magazine of a gun. The same holds true with our institutions. One nation's army, designed to protect their country, can be deployed to another part of the globe to disrupt and destroy another's. And, yes, the same holds true with our institutional thinking. Our search for genetic understanding has allowed us to make headway at combating disease, but in its perversion, we've also employed our so-called knowledge to engage in wholesale murder and genocide.

You see, even when they're intended to build and maintain the common good, our tools don't always *do* good. More accurately, we don't always employ our tools for common-good benefits. There's a reason for that. Tools, whether they are technological, institutional, or in how "we" think, have certain core qualities that cannot be designed away.

Amplification

Tools *amplify* because they have power. Power isn't inherently good or bad. What you were doing well before, you can do even better with a well-made tool. But what you were doing badly before, you can do worse. One of humanity's earliest tools was the generation and capture of fire. Humans could now cook food, but they could also lob flaming arrows at each other. Same fire. You can build a nuclear energy plant and power a city; or you could use it to create a weapon that can wipe another city off the map. It's the same technology, the same tool. And that is a pretty good reason to consider our intentions whenever we employ a tool. Effectively using a tool, technological or institutional, toward building the common good doesn't happen by accident. It happens with *common-good intent*.

Imperfection

Tools are *imperfect* because they are invented and employed by humans. And although that sounds simple, it rarely is. We tend to separate the tool from the individuals wielding them. In reality, one doesn't work with the other. Because humans are imperfect, we shouldn't expect anything we make or do to be perfect. We should expect a *better* imperfect. Computers offer a useful example of this. Over time, your computer irreparably breaks down, and you need to buy a new one. And that new computer will have more power and be able to perform more tasks more quickly than your previous one — and, if it's a laptop or tablet, it will be lighter to boot.

Not all imperfections are created equal. There are times when we need things to be as perfect as possible. We don't want our airplanes falling out of the sky. On the other hand, there are many areas where we should embrace imperfection, because that's where innovation comes from; it's where we'll discover new things. In her

2010 book, *Being Wrong*, author Kathryn Schulz observes that missing the mark, however embarrassing that can be, also allows us to develop a greater empathy for other people and for the challenges they face. Error helps to us to grow, and to not believe that the world revolves around us. It can bring us together with other imperfect people — that is, every one of us. (As I'll discuss later, screwing up is not the worst thing. Failing to learn from your screw-ups is the worst thing.) In fact, when dealing with a dynamic and ambiguous environment — like the whole world seems to be these days — seeking out quick failures, so you can learn rapidly can be an enormously effective approach.

Just like our tools' attributes of amplification should lead to some understandings about intent, the attribute of imperfection should engender a posture of *tolerance and understanding*. To err is human, and to err is also the product of our invention. To learn and move on *productively* should be part of our human journey as well.

Dislocation

Our tools *dislocate*. Our technology changes our institutions and our institutions change our technology. This has always been the case: the bigger the change, the greater the dislocation. Sometimes, those changes can be very painful. For instance, in the early fourteenth century, the use of the block and tackle (what we commonly call a pulley) came into widespread use throughout Europe. Almost overnight, a quarter of the continent's urban workers lost their jobs. These newly unemployed gathered together in marauding bands of murdering rioters. All this suffering was from what looks to be a simple pulley and a rope. Not so simple, right?

For a more recent example, take the shipping container. This simple yet remarkable invention — nothing more than a rectilinear, forty-foot-long steel box — has allowed global trade to flourish like in(tend)

never before. It has caused the cost of transportation of goods to plummet, allowing us access to a whole world of foreign-made products. But the wealth that the container has created has come with a price. The hundreds of longshoremen, who shoved and schlepped irregularly shaped agglomerations of goods, were no longer needed; neither were thousands of railroad workers. So, how much dislocation do you think is occurring with the advent of our digital communications technology? Go ask someone in the newspaper business for a quick answer.

As amplification begets the need for a focus on intent and impermanence should get us thinking about tolerance and understanding, the attribute of dislocation should direct us to consider the *implications* of a tool's introduction. What are the impacts of the tool — both good and bad?

Impermanence

Finally: Tools are *impermanent*. Some disappear, such as the wooden-handled steel hooks that longshoremen like Terry Malloy (played by Marlon Brando) used in the movie *On the Waterfront*. There are people in the world who still use stone axes, but those tools have long departed from the American construction industry's toolbox. Other tools change, often in radical and surprising ways: Think of the evolution of the telephone, from a large amplifier to a handheld smartphone (which, of course, can do far more than simply make and take calls).

No matter how far and wide you search across the globe, you cannot buy a new car with an eight-track tape player in the sound system. Were eight-tracks bad? Okay. . . they *were* kind of lame. But the point is that cassette tapes were better. And CDs better still. And even that technology is on the way out as we see more car stereo offerings that utilize MP3/MP4 players and other digital downloads. And it's quite possible that satellite linkages and mobile connections to our home music libraries may get rid of the need to bring our music with us on the road at all. And those eight-track tapes? With luck, you may be able to find them in some quirky little music or antique shop. Impermanence is as "natural" to tools as amplification, imperfection, and dislocation.

But sometimes, we become so enamored with our designs that we attempt to preserve them with little regard for their underlying service to the individuals that are supposed to be served by them. And this seems to be the case with our institutional tools more than our technologies. While we expect our technologies to be impermanent, we tend to fight against that very same attribute in our institutions. We fight against how we think of things like education, health care, and public safety. Interesting, isn't it?

These four attributes can be summarized in a phrase: *Tools are ambiguous*. Given how our tools have evolved, it's easy for many of us to believe that given enough time, they will solve all of our social ills. Certainly, that's what many believed back in the 1950s and 1960s, when American society seemed to be charging forward with the efficiency and power of a well-oiled machine — or a punch card-driven Univac (one of the first computers, for my digital-naive friends out there). These days, that faith may be a little tarnished; but many of us look upon the astonishing development of digital and medical technology and can't help but feel as our parents and grandparents did back in postwar America. Particularly when we think of the communications tools we've developed in just the past ten years, we can't help sharing, at least from time to time, the dreams of the cyber-utopians. Communications — a word whose meaning is rooted in *common* — can bring us together.

But in our more realistic moments, we know that our tools can also divide us. As we've discussed, the Internet is a tool with an unprecedented and astonishing capacity for bringing people together across all kinds of boundaries, both demographic and geographic.

It is a cornerstone of our new, networked world and a tool that has allowed us to create it. Yet, we also know that it can help us Balkanize ourselves into separate groups of likeminded people, reinforcing our prejudices and dogmas.

Our institutions have that same innate ambiguity. Take the public school, an institution that has been designed, not only for the passing on of wisdom and knowledge, but also to bring us together, to instill a common base of how we as Americans understand ourselves — in other words, as a tool to build culture. But the public school system as an institution also has proven to be socially divisive and our communities, our politicians, our teachers' unions, school superintendents, and school boards are often so attached to how our schools are currently designed that they can't see how outmoded their design is, and that this particular tool can no longer perform the task it was designed to do. (I'll talk more about the need to redesign educational institutions in the next chapter.)

Tools can (and should) be instruments of human creativity. But how they are used depends upon the human minds that control them. Tools can build. But they can also destroy. They can be used as weapons or mental crutches that actually inhibit our creativity. That's especially true when we try to hold onto our tools — and here I'm referring primarily to institutions — past the time of their usefulness.

We are all tool users, of course. But we are all toolmakers, too. That is why we need to continually reflect on the power and implications of our tools and how we employ them. Our tools have more power than ever these days. So, a crucial issue for us now is to evaluate their designs and to use them for the common good, which is how any tool should be intended, after all.

All this raises a question that we've been dancing around: What *is* the common good? That question in itself is a battleground. The advocacy groups I discussed in the previous chapter use communication devices and other tools as weapons within the temples of conflict, in their fund-raising requests to their constituents, and on the Internet to assert that what they are fighting for is what will be good for all of us. But as we've noted, these groups are fighting mostly for the insular good — for particular interests against other interests.

But if we strip away the one-sided rhetoric and all the use and misuse of tools, we'll uncover something that may surprise many of us — and make us more hopeful of our future.

What we'll uncover is not a battleground, but common ground.

A Mind-set is a tool?

I know it is strange to consider a mere mind-set as a tool, but think about it this way as applied to institutions. If you wanted to think about something as an "article of faith," you'd be employing a certain way of thinking. And similarly, there is a "business way" of thinking about a challenge, wouldn't you agree?

Sometimes, it's useful to look at something and say, "How can I make money at this?" That's called a business mind-set, and being compensated is important for no other reason than it shows that you created something that was of sustained value to others. Commerce is important and we must not forget that. Allowing people to be productive and compensated are incredibly important elements of a place where you'd want to hang out and live.

So, having a mind-set of creating value for others produces important opportunities. And it all starts with a mind-set of a "way" of thinking, a way of pointing you to other tools, so you can analyze the opportunity. A pretty powerful tool in my estimation!

mind(set)

Why Do We Weaponize Our Tools First?

I'm guessing that the first of our ancestors who captured fire didn't invite the neighbors over for some tasty mastodon on a bed of field greens, perhaps with a side of lentils and nice Chianti to wash it down. No, probably more often, our ancestors weren't preparing for an Iron Age Chef competition on the Prehistoric Food Network. They were throwing some of that fire in the neighboring tribe's faces to scare them off, so that they could enjoy all that yummy beast themselves. It seems that so many of our inventions are first used in that manner.

Here's a pretty dramatic example:

In a desolate corner of the New Mexican desert on July 16, 1945, the first nuclear weapons test of an atomic bomb, called Trinity, was successfully accomplished. Weeks later, on August 6 and 9, atomic bombs were dropped on the Japanese cities of Hiroshima and Nagasaki, respectively. It was nearly nine years later when the Soviet Union's Obninsk Nuclear Power Plant became the world's first tool utilizing atomic energy to put electricity onto the power grid for human benefit. The United States' first commercial nuclear power plant came four years later, on May 26, 1958, when President Dwight Eisenhower opened the Shippingport Nuclear Power plant in Pennsylvania. Interestingly enough, the power facility was part of Eisenhower's "Atoms for Peace" program. And while we now know that there are peaceful uses for the atom, we are still left with the original ability and threat of our capacity to kill one another with that power.

Yes, I guess it's technically true: Guns don't kill people, people do. But why is it that so often we have to get a gruesome act out of the way before we repurpose our tools for human benefit?

The Naked Eight

A BIG REASON DISCUSSING THE common good — rather than vociferously arguing about it — has become so difficult is because, instead of *addressing* the attributes of a strong, healthy community, we're fixating on how those attributes are *dressed*.

What do I mean by this? Take education, for example. We can all agree that education — the passing on of knowledge and wisdom from one generation to the next — is an attribute of a healthy community. But when we focus on how this attribute is dressed — in other words, what education should "look like" — the disagreements begin: disagreement that can explode into disagreeability — angry conflict.

As I've noted, we tend to focus on the tool rather than the outcome. When we think education, we think less about wisdom and knowledge (the outcome) and more about schools, teachers, and curricula (the tools).

If we're going to make true progress on any of the issues that we face as a society, we need to look beyond the tools. To interweave another metaphor: We need to remove the old clothing of our pre-conceptions, prejudices, and opinions, stripping naked down to the essential attributes of the common good. I believe that these characteristics are much easier for nearly all of us to agree upon than how to achieve them. Once we see the common good with naked clarity, we can then discuss how to use and design our tools.

I call the attributes of a common-good society that we can agree upon the Naked Eight. Simply put, we thrive in communities where:

1. People feel SAFE
2. People experience good HEALTH
3. People are PRODUCTIVE
4. People are COMPENSATED
5. People can INNOVATE
6. People live in a good ENVIRONMENT, both built and preserved
7. People can pass on KNOWLEDGE
8. People can enjoy JUSTICE

If you'll let my metaphor clash a little: We can best understand Naked Eight as threads. They are not separate from each other — they are interwoven. Lose one thread, and a hole emerges in a community's supportive fabric — it's not truly and fully a common-good community. If a child isn't well fed, doesn't feel safe, or lives in a home or goes to a school that's falling apart, he or she will be discouraged from learning. And our community will have lost a happy, productive, creative citizen — to the loss and detriment of us all.

It might not sound as though eight threads would make up much of a fabric. In fact, each attribute is constructed from many fibers. For instance, our environment is both built — the infrastructure that makes up our transportation systems, energy distribution, tele-communications, and so on. And it is unbuilt (though, often, still maintained) — nature, parks, clean water, and air. The environment is in itself a fabric, and its elements are inseparable. To visit a national park, you need a way to get there. A well-maintained infrastructure is essential to the common good, in large part because it aids us in coming together — to commute, to commune, and to be in community.

We can best understand Naked Eight as threads. They are not separate from each other — they are interwoven. Lose one thread, and a hole emerges in a community's supportive fabric.

Because the Naked Eight are so tightly interwoven, we can focus mostly on one of them, touching upon the interconnections here and there. Many of the points we can make of one apply to all. Take education. In our nation, there are plenty of schools, and certainly innumerable teachers, doing a fine job of passing on wisdom and knowledge to the next generation. Still, the overall data are irrefutable: Too many children aren't graduating, and even among those who have, too many aren't prepared for productive, happy adult lives. They haven't been taught how to *keep learning*. (Assuming, that is, that they've been truly and fully taught to learn at all.)

We can point to many reasons for the sad state of American education. But the overarching one is this (and here I'm drawing from the insights of British education reformer Sir Ken Robinson): The majority of our schools are the product of an out-of-date design. Look at the typical classroom. It has been designed for an industrial-age economy. Students are in rows, face forward: I talk, you listen, and don't fidget. There are the absorption of facts to be tested, the measurement of goals to be reached, and the standards to be met. Then, there are the bells that sound to mark the end of each "shift."

In short, education has become in many ways an industry that isn't so much about the passing on of knowledge and wisdom as it is, unfortunately, about the tools of education and the politics that surround it.

Daniel Pink, the author of *A Whole New Mind, Drive* and many other great pieces of writing, tells how he received all A's in his four years of studying French in high school — and yet is unable to speak French fluently. While there are language immersion programs here and there in the U.S., by and large, our kids aren't taught to be French *speakers*. They're taught to be French *students*. I myself earned a law degree, but I didn't learn how to be a lawyer — I learned how to be a law student. Ask any lawyer (I'm not one, by the way) and I bet they'll tell you that they learned how to be a lawyer when they actually started practicing.

Then there's the summer vacation, which slows down our children's learning — in a very real sense, kids need to relearn how to learn at the beginning of the school year. Interestingly, while the structure of the classroom follows an established, industrial-age design, the structure of the school year follows a traditional agricultural model. Students get the entire summer off in memory of the time when children were expected to help in the fields. These days, in many states, it isn't necessarily the agricultural industry that is keeping summers off into law. It's the resorts. Their lobby is the one that's saying, "You can't start a school day before Labor Day because we'll lose our business." And while we may not be totally unsympathetic to their interests and value to vacationing families, it's legitimate to ask what their impact is on our larger societal goals.

I'm not suggesting, of course, that we shouldn't have schools (or even a short summer vacation). Of course, we should. But the curriculum and its delivery of that curriculum must change. Being "classically educated" is an ideal that works wonderfully well for a small group of students. But for most, it isn't very relevant and valuable in what this world is looking like right now. The whole idea of having a model based on acquisition — you have to prove to me that you can regurgitate this book of knowledge and then you get some letters after your name — is less valuable than: Show me you know how to apply this knowledge in a new situation that hasn't occurred yet. What's more valuable in the twenty-first century?

In summary: Contemporary education is working off of a design — an outmoded design, a caricature of a design, really — that is built for the tool and not for human beings. To again quote Daniel Pink: "Our schools should be preparing our children for *their* future, not for *our* past." And here's another pertinent quotation — this one ascribed to the legendary philosopher of ancient China, Laozi (whose name is more familiar to us in English as Lao-Tzu). To me, it still best expresses the most successful "methodology" of education: "Tell me something, and I'll forget it; show it to me, and I'll remember it; have me do it, and I'll understand it." Current studies of brain science are underscoring Laozi's wisdom. The current model of education is a highly inefficient and out-of-date way to teach students, so that they'll actually absorb and creatively use knowledge and wisdom. Oh, and by the way, that sage philosopher said this thousands of years ago. This isn't exactly new thinking.

Indeed, we used to teach people in ways that were much more practical. We used to call these activities apprenticeships and guilds. But now, we have a system instead that is built on a model that we know does not encourage learning. If I talk and you listen, you'll get maybe 50 percent of that (some studies suggest that it's probably less). If I show you something, you'll retain much more. But if I have you do it, then you will truly understand and be able to apply it.

I'll happily use myself as an example. I was taught math in a way that I just could not relate to. If you ask me what the difference is between 1/8th and 1/16th, I will surely hesitate. But if you were to show it to me on a snare drum, I'd never forget it. Different delivery design, better outcome.

Want to see this approach in action? Consider the cadets who have been attending the U.S. Air Force Academy the past few years. They astonish their instructors with their eye-hand coordination as they react and maneuver their controls and their ability to process multiple points of data with seeming simultaneity. They have abilities that would leave previous generations of cadets in the dust. A good thing for their superiors: These newer cadets can operate the high-tech fighter planes and ancillary weapon support systems that typify modern defense. Their amazing capabilities didn't come from sitting in a classroom, eyes snapped forward, while instructors droned on. Those talents were honed in hours and hours of the immersive experience of electronic gaming. They weren't being told — they were *doing*.

Does this mean we should convert all of our schools into gaming arcades? Of course not. Clearly, students need structure, and how well (or how badly) they're learning needs to be measured. But we should be asking: Are *all of* our children truly being educated in ways that will help them and their communities? Will they come out of school with the wisdom and knowledge they'll need to be productive, healthy, and happy? Will they know how to think, so that they can respond creatively, calmly, and mindfully to the changes that are coming toward us all with such speed? (And will they learn how to respond thoughtfully to the Outrage Industry and the Angertainers?) Are we asking of them, not just how intelligent they are, but rather, how ARE they intelligent?

So, the argument isn't: Blow up our schools! Nor is it: I learned in a highly-structured school environment, and if it was good enough for me, it's good enough for these kids who aren't learning. There is no argument that learning should be structured — the question is to the structure itself. But we can acknowledge that our schools, as most of them are currently designed, are failing too many communities. And it's important to point out that a badly-designed education system isn't very fair to all the hard-working people associated with

in(action)

teaching our kids. Once again: It's an example of good people working in a dysfunctional design.

Defenders of the status quo need to understand that people have changed. Our society has changed. The traditional public school structure might have worked well when we needed millions of men to work on the assembly line or millions of office workers pushing paper. But that tool is no longer a good design when today's charge is to teach people to think creatively and innovatively. The old world is passing away. And that's precisely what's making a lot of people anxious and angry.

By the way, it's not just traditionalists who want to preserve that traditional structure. Teachers' unions, which aren't considered conservative entities, also have a great deal invested in the current dominant design. Certainly, many teachers would like to see some changes, and some of them are exhibiting a lot of courage in the face of the defenders of the status quo — oftentimes, that means their unions — as they push for transformation. But certain ideas — firing non-performing teachers, for instance, or providing public support of charter schools and other innovations — can cause them to throw barricades around the bureaucracy of public education, a design they can use as a protective fortification.

Yes, there certainly are pockets of innovation emerging in education. The point is that we have not fully acculturated those ideas and those technologies and those opportunities because we are still wrapped up on the powerful tool of our thinking of what a school is, how it gets financed, and who has to go to it and when. We are still distracted by the arguments around the powerful political persuasions of the institutions that are publicly funded. We've made precious little progress on improving how we pass on knowledge and wisdom because we are wrapped up in talk about our tools and the politics around them. So, it becomes a matter not of how much you've learned, but of how much time your butt was in a seat. And that dictate goes well beyond the power of a teachers' union. Our official accrediting bodies, the folks who determine what can legally be defined as education, are continuing to foist this traditional model on educators themselves. The issue is a lot more complex than our common education debates would let on.

So, in order to make education relevant in the world as it is now, we must redesign. But even as we do so, we must build on existing foundations. After all, we're *passing on* knowledge, not reinventing it. And that points to something crucial about achieving a common-good design: It's not a matter of doing one thing OR the other. It's doing one thing AND the other. That's an important point I'll return to later.

If we focused not on schools, but on education itself, we would have an easier time imagining, creating, and constructing new designs. These designs could include, for instance, entertainment arts and digital technology, with all the immersive engagement of Sim City, Second Life, or Rock Band. In fact, these kinds of approaches and technologies are already emerging. But we still have a mind-set where we don't commonly call electronic gaming a form of education. We should.

Feeling Safe? Enough?

Just as we default to the Industrial Revolution model of education, something similar happens when we talk about public safety: We default to cops and judges and security cameras and jails. When we let our minds go to default positions, that's when the common-good attribute becomes a political issue, and then become subject to demagoguery, bad politics, and the Outrage Industry.

Yet, despite or because of all the "security" and "safety" measures we've put in place — particularly since 9/11 — the United States has the largest number of prisoners per capita in the developed world.

That's expensive. What's more, it doesn't build the common good and that means our society and many of our fellow citizens aren't flourishing. If we look solely at the tools that we've gotten used to employing to ensure security, we won't see other ways to create a safe environment that would actually be more beneficial. What about good lighting, for instance? What about the ways that buildings, streets, and sidewalks can be laid out, so that there are "eyes on the street"? That is, what about the existing (and underused) methods that allow and encourage residents to keep an eye on what's going on in outdoor public spaces? How about taking advantage of proven ways that encourage neighbors to interact with each other like National Night Out and thus discourage crime? Once again, how do we become actors who produce a better outcome?

Even then, safety and security can't truly and fully exist without the other Naked Eight attributes. How well are the community's schools doing their job? How are the community's health and dietary habits? Is its public infrastructure well maintained? Unless we address all the attributes, the tools we use to address a single attribute — no matter how good those tools are — will provide only quick fixes … at best.

Better approaches won't be simple and they shouldn't be. These aren't simple challenges, after all. But our approaches and our designs could stand to be a lot more creative. We live in one of the most dynamic eras of all times. The scale of change is enormous and the pace of it is ever quickening. Whether we move incrementally or in large leaps, we are going to have to re-imagine ourselves creatively as we redesign around the Naked Eight. The Naked Eight provide ways to fresh thinking. Producing those opportunities with creativity will be particularly important currently because of the nature of all these changes: What got us here isn't what is going to get us into a better tomorrow. And that creativity is going to have to be practiced everywhere — in our schools, our hospitals, our governments, and our businesses.

Finally, a word on optimism. A common-good place has an optimistic mind-set undergirding it all. This optimism is intertwined with the care and concern we have for each other. A community with optimism rebuilds after a flood, and it redesigns. Without optimism, the dam is never rebuilt — or at best, it's rebuilt badly. And to build or rebuild well, whether it's a dam, a school, or an entire community, means choosing our tools with care. That is, with the Naked Eight first and foremost.

 What got us here isn't what is going to get us into a better tomorrow.

The Naked Eight elements are what should always be most relevant to our societal attention and to what we design toward. Later on, we'll discuss how that focus on social relevance can be used in how we produce more successful and prosperous communities.

But even optimism isn't enough to untangle one of the most tightly-knotted complexities of the common good. As we begin to redesign, there is a crucial distinction that we must understand, or else our work will end in profound disappointment. And we'll be thrown back once again into the us-versus-them mind-set we're trying to overcome.

We have to understand that there are many challenges we simply won't be able to solve once and for all. Read on and you'll see why that's the case.

The World Is Pretty Complex ... Eight, Really?

Well, other people may have more than eight and some may describe this concept differently. Sometimes, it's best to undesign before we go about redesigning. Stripping down to the Naked Eight is an undesign mind-set that allows us to gather around those things that we rarely if ever argue about. Think about that. There are things that we don't argue about! Where do you find the argument about the need to educate ourselves? Where do you find the argument about the need to live in safety? Where do you find the argument that we need to have a healthy and vibrant economy? The Naked Eight represents the root imperatives of what makes the kind of place you'd like to hang out in and maybe raise a family. These are the arenas around which we build institutions, technologies, and rules. These are the arenas where we regulate all those threads for our general benefit ... where we make it all work better. Not perfect, but better. Eight things aren't too many to remember, are they?

HIGHER ED IS NO LONGER JUST A LECTURE HALL

"Whoever started the trend that 'going to get your education' was synonymous with going to school, should be kicked in the ass."

This sentence resonates with me for two reasons. First, it's funny. Second, it's *almost* spot on. To be honest, I'm not ready to completely throw in the towel on higher ed. This provocation is from a piece on the website Under30CEO.com titled *Finding the Education of an Entrepreneur*. Before I go any further, I'd like to note that I myself attended college and graduate school, along with many of my fellow entrepreneur friends. So, this is no bash on higher education; it's simply a statement that reflects the reality of a world that has changed a lot since I sat in a classroom. And that statement is that now, in the twenty-first century, getting your education is a whole lot more than sitting in a sterile lecture hall with seventy-nine other sleepy students, while your professor drones on about the education *they're* trying to give *you*. Simply put, education just can't be that passive in a world that, not only has changed *dramatically*, but also is changing *constantly*.

So, in addition to sitting in that classroom (because the marketplace still puts some value on getting formal letters after your name), getting your education should be attributed to those books you read before you fall asleep at night, or your thirty-day backpacking trip around South America. It should be attributed to the TED talks you watch online, that "Oh my, is that cool!" idea you grabbed from Pop!Tech and your several failed attempts at creating the newest social networking site. More and more, education isn't just about learning how to apply yesterday's learning to today; it's about doing things — TODAY. It's about finding your interest — whether it is equestrian science or carbon dating — and getting out there to learn about it, to get your hands dirty, and to network your butt out in your field of interest. Folks, there has NEVER, EVER been so much knowledge at your fingertips, and if you think that you can glean it by merely being a passive spectator, you'll miss out on one of the greatest attributes of this digital age.

I'm not saying college is overrated *per se*, but I am saying that higher ed alone will not get you where you want to go; you need to find your education in alternative — and often times unexpected — places. Be strategically INEFFICIENT when it comes to where you think you can learn something.

You never know what you'll pick up and apply to your path. And what you never take the time to learn about ... you'll never know, right?

The Problem with Problem Solving

BUILDING THE COMMON GOOD — or weaving it, if you will — is *not* a matter of solving a number of discrete problems. Oh, if only it were that simple!

By definition, once a problem is solved, it's solved once and for all. Add one to one, and the answer is always two, forever. (Unless you're a visual thinker like me and come up with eleven ... because it looks that way. Have I told you I was bad at math?) Indeed, you can consider mathematics one of humanity's greatest tools. The use of Arabic numerals was once termed "algorism," a term that evolved into the word algorithm. Simply defined, an algorithm is a process for solving a problem in a set series of steps. And it gives consistent, predictable results. You put in the inputs — one plus one — and the result is a predictable two. Problem solved! For good! Too often, that's how many of us look at the challenges of building and maintaining a common-good society. Give us the right tools, technologies, and institutions, and we can solve any challenge that comes our way. Plug in the right inputs, and we'll achieve the right outcomes, the right solutions. *Voilà!*

It's a mentality that's planted deep into our mythology, the notion of American know-how. And as I've noted, during the post-World War II era, that mythology did seem to "work," as American scientists and businesses created one astonishing innovation after another: polymer plastics, computers, transistors, and semiconductors. Perhaps that perspective is one of the factors that has given Sudden Illumination Syndrome its power: We have revealed an underlying nervous notion that we no longer have that mythologized ability to solve any challenge that comes our way. That's pretty tough, especially these days, when we can see a tsunami of challenges headed our way.

I hope I've already convinced you that throughout our history, we humans have shown ourselves to be fantastic toolmakers. Whether it's mathematic formulas, iPads, public education, the Green Revolution, heart valves, or communications satellites, we have a right to be proud of our capability for invention and innovation. But there's one thing we humans have never been good at: perfection. And we'll never be able to produce it. "Perfect," by definition, means complete, without faults or drawbacks. As discussed in the previous chapter, our tools aren't perfect, and never will be. Show me a perfect human being, and I'll show you someone who's capable of producing the perfect tool.

Yet, we still cling to the notion that, over time, we can find all the right algorithms that will allow us to operate our businesses, society, and life with a predictable regularity. This mentality is certainly common in business and government throughout our recent history. During the postwar boom years of the early to mid-1960s, economists like Walter Heller and Arthur Okun believed that with the scientifically precise mix of monetary and tax policies, economic cycles could be regulated as effectively as a building's heating and cooling system. More recently, the inventors of complex financial instruments like derivatives, mortgage-backed securities, and collateralized debt obligations were supremely confident that they had finally found the right formulae for hedging all risk. And the only perfect thing that produced was a perfect mess, right?

 There's one thing we humans have never been good at: perfection.

Over and over again, we've had to learn the same lesson: There is no such thing as a tool for eternity. A master plumber can fix your sink, so that it won't need fixing for decades. But someday, it will need to be re-repaired. The oxygen and water that keep us alive also wear away at pipes and ducts. Roads will always develop potholes. Computer circuitry will always malfunction. As our knowledge increases and we design new technologies, how we educate ourselves will naturally need to be updated.

The point is this: Common-good challenges are not problems to be solved. They are *dilemmas*. A dilemma is a challenge that never goes away, that's never "solved" once and for all. Dilemmas can only be *managed*, every day. Shifting from "problem" to "dilemma" isn't merely a quick turn of a word. You put very different strategies in place when you're facing an ongoing dilemma.

 Common-good challenges are not problems to be solved. They are dilemmas.

We can see the dynamic of dilemmas in action through the lens of the Naked Eight. Look at the attribute of safety. You will most likely never live in a crime-free community. As I referred to in the last chapter, when we think about crime, we might think about jails and the institutions of a court system and police. But these tools, no matter how well managed, don't really "solve" the problem of crime. As mentioned before, the United States has the highest incarceration rate in the developed world. But it also has the highest level of crimes involving guns. So, if you really want to manage the dilemma of a safe community, you need to look at other tools as well, such as streetscapes, schools, and the health of the economy. If we simply look at safety as merely adding more cops and think we'll magically get rid of all the robbers and other criminals, we will actually have robbed ourselves of more creative approaches that can lead us to communities that are truly safer.

True, those who can afford to do so can live in a gated development. That solves the problem for *them*. But they aren't living in a *common*-good community. They're simply insulating themselves. And even at that, there's always the nagging dilemma of domestic violence, which knows no economic boundary, nor respects a gate around a neighborhood of mansions. No, wherever your address, you probably don't live in a crime-free community. But that doesn't mean you can't live in a safer community. And a safer community is an ongoing effort: a dilemma.

As a Population, We Will Never Be in "Perfect" Health

Or take another Naked Eight attribute: health. Many of us believe that government and laws can "fix" the problem of bad health. We can pass laws against soda pop, for instance — or, of course, for greater access to the health care system, which is really access to sick care. Or, looking at it from the other side of the spectrum, we can loosen regulations to allow medical devices and pharmaceuticals that supposedly will "fix" certain physical problems to come more quickly to market. And while all of these approaches may in and of themselves have merit, we will never live in a community where everyone is healthy.

Why? Because our bodies aren't machines. A knee replacement, for instance, isn't the same as getting new brake pads for your Volvo. Orthopedic surgery changes how your body operates — it improves the situation, but your new knee isn't the same as the old one. And in twenty years (assuming you live that long), it will have to be replaced again. (So, of course, will those brake pads.)

Likewise, health care. There will always be sick people out there. Minds will succumb to schizophrenia or autism spectrum disorders. Babies will be born with congenital afflictions. Our environments will be rife with viruses and bacteria. Someone suffering from a rare "orphan disease" like swallowing syncope (which causes the sufferer's heart to stop beating every time he or she swallows) can tell you how difficult it was to understand what was happening to them, and how many years it took to get a diagnosis. And even then, there's no cure — only ways to manage the disease.

Then, there is the problem — a dilemma, really — of medical error: It's estimated that human mistakes in the hospital kill more people each year than AIDS or breast cancer. And that is because no matter how "perfect" our medical science is, the application of it, doctoring, is the practice of an imperfect art. Like the human body itself, the health care system is far too complex to be reduced to the simple terms of problems and fixes. It *can't* be fixed.

So, what can we do to face these dilemmas? Actually, a great deal.

First, we need to acknowledge that imperfection. We have to acknowledge that the tools and designs we have in place can't be made perfect, and that they need to be constantly analyzed and adjusted. In some cases, we need to create new designs and new tools. If we don't acknowledge that permanent imperfection, we forgo the need for a feedback loop and we close off the possibility of improvement, and of responding creatively to these dilemmas. Once we start thinking in terms of dilemmas and not problems, we can ask: "How are our tools and designs working? What unintended consequences are they creating?" And once we have the intellectual honesty to have those conversations, then we should have the freedom and creativity to redesign, not only our technologies, but our institutions as well.

Second, we need to see that better is as perfect as we'll get — and that better can be very good. In fact, I'd put it this way: Be proud of better — and be suspicious of "perfect."

We also need to acknowledge that since we live in a permanently imperfect world, we can't look at the common-good attributes in binary terms — as zero or one, or black or white. Our communities are neither safe nor unsafe; we're neither healthy nor unhealthy. But we can be safer, and we can be healthier. We can always improve.

Very simply, if we don't acknowledge those imperfections, whether in our tools or in our ways of thinking, we will be unable to improve our communities. This is why compromise is so important — and so hard to achieve. Both sides of an issue believe that they have the "solution" to any given social problem. If you believe in perfection, then compromise is a shortcoming, almost a moral failing — a sign that you're less than fully committed to your beliefs and values. And, of course, you're also more likely to cling to the tools associated with those values.

 Be proud of better — and be suspicious of "perfect."

The myth of American know-how has instilled in many of us a blind optimism about the future, while Sudden Illumination Syndrome has imparted the queasy sensation that the future may not be better than the past or present. We nervously question everything, thinking that the future may well be worse!

To be sure, underlying the Naked Eight common-good attributes is optimism. But for optimism to be truly good and useful, it must

affix

look ahead with open eyes. It must understand our limitations as well as our capabilities. Psychologists use a concept called "optimism bias" to describe a blind faith in the future. The latest recession was the product of that bias.

Yet, neither should we despair. Realism is what's needed. History is filled with numerous grim examples of people and societies that believed that they could achieve a machine-like perfection. All have ended disastrously. If we look at the rise of communism, fascism, and their various mutations, we see that the citizens of those nations let themselves become passive. Those societies divided, not only into spectators and actors, but spectators and dictators.

But once we begin to think in terms of dilemmas and better-as-perfect, we actually can make common-good societies better than if we tried to achieve perfection.

By releasing ourselves from the idea of pure perfection, we can become less enamored of our tools. This allows us to focus instead on our fellow human beings — the very people whom our tools need to be designed for. A dilemma mind-set allows us the benefits of creativity and redesign. And that new perspective just might release us from the inane politics of defense and defensiveness around our tools. It allows for forgiveness for our missteps, and for repair. It allows us empathy. And it allows a more humane approach to addressing our dilemmas — one that is more flexible, more active, and much more creative.

One of the drawbacks of a politicized approach to the common good is, as we've discussed, the dominance of advocacy groups in common-good policy. We let ourselves become spectators as they perform their angertainment. Advocacy groups thrive both on uncertainty (notably, our fears) and on certainty — the certainty that their ideas and "solutions" are absolutely right, and that "the other side" is absolutely wrong. And too often, advocates weaponize their "truth" by allowing perfection to be the enemy of the good enough, preventing compromise and engendering ever more political gridlock.

What's more, many of these groups are purposefully blind to unintended consequences. They're too busy defending the tool and the approach. Take welfare. Our society certainly needs to provide a safety net — it's an attribute of the common good. But welfare is a tool that should be used along with other tools, so that recipients ultimately no longer need it. Productivity, purpose, and compensation also are Naked Eight attributes. But welfare, as it has often been structured, works against those attributes. And many welfare advocates have become so protective of the tool that they've become blind to what the tool is supposed to accomplish.

And we all become blind to the fact that a common-good approach to social challenges requires more than one kind of tool. With that in mind, let's take a look at one of the most widely used and misused tools in the current state of the art of common-good design, and one that, perhaps above others, has turned citizens into spectators of the common good: government regulation.

Life versus Living: Which Is the Best Path to Death?

A number of years ago, my dad and I joined a few friends up in Alaska for salmon fishing. Salmon are amazing creatures. Born in river streams, they swim out to the ocean for several years and then come back to the very same river to spawn a new generation. They enter the river shiny and beautiful, lay or inseminate eggs — and then they begin to die. They become disfigured, their colors change, and they literally rot on the bone. One of my new-to-salmon-fishing friends looked at this with horror and asked our guide what was wrong with the fish. Our guide chuckled and said, "There is absolutely nothing wrong with them. They have lived their lives and now, having produced another generation, they are dying. There is nothing 'wrong' with them."

Unlike those beautiful salmon, humans have produced a bevy of tools to prolong life in many situations where, if left to nature, we would die — sooner. We now are given the choice to hang onto life by a few threads if only so we can be present in this world a little longer. And by present, I mean just barely alive. Under the current state of the art, we all still die. Death is not an option — but delaying it can be.

Given that we're all going to end up there, it would seem that it's particularly important to openly discuss end-of-life options, both with family and with doctors. The reason this is important is because you need to make a difficult decision: Do you live *longer* or live *better*? Do you live out your last few days as a coherent human being, knowing your time has almost come, therefore allowing you to make the most out of it? Or do you stretch out your time for another several weeks, even if conversations might not be optimal and contentedness might be minimal?

Here's something fascinating and counterintuitive: the Center for Disease Control and other outfits are coming out with findings that those who've entered hospice and had palliative care — that is, those who had the chance to have meaningful conversations with their family and caregivers about pain control and the quality of their last days — actually lived longer. Yes, they still died. And the point isn't even that they lived a few weeks longer. The thing we should focus on is that they lived better before they died.

This goes back to my thoughts about sick-care transactions and dilemmas. Nowadays, death may seem like it is optional, but is hanging on at any cost (financial and emotionally) really the best option if you're not really *living*? At some point perhaps, we should start thinking of death less as a matter of a non-preventable sickness medical transaction and start thinking of it more as health habitat interaction between people and their community at one of the most important and meaningful parts of their lives: their exits.

This is not to argue one bit against the amazing strides we have made in our curative abilities. These worthy endeavors have not only brought longevity to many. More importantly, they've provided better quality of life to those who otherwise would not have had it. But as a good friend of mine once said, "You could cure cancer and there'd still be a leading cause of death." Even now, there is a point where every one of us will die. Some will live long, others will have their lives cut tragically short, some will experience blessedly little morbidity and suffering before they pass, and others will unfortunately experience a far less pain-free end of their lives. Yet, the very end is still the same.

It's an old and true saying that adding years to the life is not as important as adding life to the years. Perhaps if we understood the difference between the act of delaying death and the practice of extending life, especially when we are focusing on the qualities that make up a life, we will start putting the same effort into palliative care and designing hospice health habitats as we have into prevent-death-at-any-cost medical transactions.

Re-Regulating Regulation

IN THE 1930S WITH THE NEW DEAL and again in the 1960s with the Great Society, the United States made tremendous strides in how we used the tool of government to meet the needs of the common good. It's worth reciting the list of these amalgams of federal legislation's splendid accomplishments: Social Security, the Securities and Exchange Commission, federal backing of home mortgages, and Medicare and Medicaid. And although it wasn't part of the New Deal as such, the passage of the GI Bill (officially, the Servicemen's Readjustment Act of 1944) was driven by the same spirit. The legislation opened the doors of higher education to millions of men who otherwise couldn't have afforded it — and helped drive postwar America's spectacular and unprecedentedly broad foundation of innovation and prosperity.

The New Deal and the Great Society forged powerfully good tools. And like all tools, they were powerfully imperfect. In seeking to solve some of our society's greatest social challenges — and, to be sure, making great improvements in the process — the New Deal, and its child of the 1960s, the Great Society, also created new dilemmas.

Most notably, they significantly changed our institutional thinking, and in some significantly unproductive ways. The success and popularity of their programs were such that more and more Americans began to think of themselves less as citizens of a participatory democratic republic and more like taxpaying customers of government. We professionalized public service, shifting it to the domain of politicians, bureaucrats, and a unionized public workforce. And that professionalization has changed the way we interact with each other and even how we think of our government. You even see this in how we refer to this important tool: "The" government comes off our lips far more often than "our" government.

 Americans began to think of themselves less as citizens of a participatory democratic republic and more like taxpaying customers of government.

We now tend to think: "I no longer have to be my brother's keeper because my taxes pay for a government program who hires someone to take care of my brother." We can leave the caretaking of the common good to the professionals and experts with their specialized degrees, leaving us to live lives as workers and consumers, and less as citizens. And along the way, as we constructed a world with more prominent government and we began to affix more and more laws and regulations upon government, like tools attached to a Swiss Army knife. That's because we came to believe that this is the way society runs: through governmental laws and regulations.

It's not that laws are bad; again, laws can be powerfully good. The rule of law is one of the pillars of the healthy interactions and transactions in a free society. The issue is that we have trained ourselves to think that passing laws is the *only* way to create predictability and accountability — that is, how we regulate our institutions and ourselves with the aim of producing the common good. Laws and regulations are our algorithms; and if any of them doesn't quite work well, government should pass *more* laws and regulations. Consciously or unconsciously, we have become accustomed to thinking of laws and government as the only real tools in the common-good toolbox.

But are laws good *enough*? There are some significant difficulties with relying too much on laws as our regulatory preference.

One is that laws are created in temples of conflict — the legislative halls of our capitols. And there's a design problem within that. Our capitols operate on a legislative system that is designed for adversarialism. As I've noted before, it's a great design when the conversation is around a policy, where you're black and I'm white, we argue and horse-trade, and we get to gray. It's a really bad design when the conversation is all about politics — positioning, posturing, pandering to the base, and black and white get hurt if they try to achieve that gray.

What's more, laws often don't regulate behavior very well at all, except in a limited, negative way. A U.S. Representative from Minnesota in the 1910s named Andrew J. Volstead once declared, "Law does regulate morality." He used this phrase to justify his introduction to the enabling legislation for the Eighth Amendment to the U.S. Constitution, better known as Prohibition. We all know how well that particular piece of legislation "regulated" morality. That law almost singlehandedly created a whole new criminal class, one that's still a scourge in many urban areas. Powerful tool, huh?

It might seem bizarre to us now that Prohibition could ever have been enshrined in the Constitution. But the idea had many supporters

— and for many of those supporters, the driving impulse was to create healthier communities (particularly healthier communities of industrial workers). But just as we can't simply pass laws to make us more "moral," we can't pass laws to make us healthier. You can pass laws that *might* encourage that. You can make fast-food restaurants show their caloric counts; you can follow the City of San Francisco's lead and make it illegal for McDonald's to sell Happy Meals with a free toy. (You can still buy Happy Meals in nearby municipalities, however, and in San Francisco, McDonald's charges a dime for the toy.) You could charge people to ride the escalator instead of taking the stairs. But do we really think that these prohibitions, these legislative designs, are going to make us that much healthier as a whole? Or are we really seeing politicians and certain interest groups putting points on the scoreboard? If we want healthier communities, we will need other tools. And we need all of our tools working together in such a way that turns us as active participants toward those goals.

A World That Is Starting to Operate as a Whole World

There's one last key thing to point to when we consider the design problem with over relying on laws, one we'll explore later on: Laws are the function of physical political jurisdictions. And increasingly, we live in a world that doesn't operate that way. We live in a world that looks like a *whole* world. We've globalized with connections and actions that literally span the planet on a minute-by-minute basis. Our world has become more mobile, yet we are still trying to regulate it in a very immobile way. Take global finance and the recent economic turmoil as an example: The technology of money and its various instruments — not only stocks and bonds, but derivatives, mortgage-backed securities, credit default swaps, and synthetic collateralized debt obligations, and so on — flowed globally. Yet, there does not exist a legal framework that could hope to regulate the geographic totality of that activity. The result was that in 2008, money gushed out of global markets with little ability to cap it.

The point here is that the physical and economic health of our country and the communities that comprise it don't require better government. But they do require better *governance*. Or rather, they require better government, *AND* better businesses, *AND* better nonprofits, *AND* every other sector you can think of. They all need to be working together — by design.

"By design" not only means that common-good intent is intrinsic to their activities; it also means playing to those various sectors' strengths. Every one of those sectors is designed to do something really good. Businesses, at their best, are good at serving paying customers. Government, particularly at the federal level is less efficient by design — i.e., we really don't want it to be too efficient (although few of us would complain if it were just a little more). And that is because government has a pretty heavy load — to serve everyone. Nonprofits aren't profit motivated — they have a mission. Every sector not only has its own design — each has its own "coins of the realm." Businesses seek money, nonprofits seek members, religious orders seek worshippers, and politicians seek votes. There are all sorts of ways that we assign support to institutions and the actors within them.

These institutions, these tools, all have special attributes. Better governance means getting those attributes to work well together to create that common-good outcome. There isn't a challenge in our world that isn't filled with complexity and where it would be just plain unwise to say, "This one sector can handle the entire load." Yet, we still look to individual sectors, especially government, for our salvation and complain bitterly when it disappoints.

We don't honor a tool by overusing it or using it in ways that it really wasn't designed to do. We wouldn't expect our nonprofits to handle our community's policing needs. We wouldn't expect our businesses to be out there running churches. But too often, we quickly turn to government as the universal tool for nearly every repair. Quite frankly, if you're like me and truly appreciate government and what it takes to utilize that complex tool, it's not a very fair way for us to treat something so important.

So, here's the new deal: When it comes to the common good and creating better designs around the Naked Eight attributes, we need to talk about something beside and beyond the political system. We need to address how our institutions will work together and thrive rather than merely survive. We need to think about other places in society where we can engage each other in less adversarial and angry conversations. And we need to think about how we can create accountability to the common good in ways that don't require the often-blunt instrument of a law. When we look outside of our normal, angry processes, we'll see that many, perhaps even most, of our country's greatest common-good successes were not products of laws alone, but of changes in our habits and the culture that we produced to better honor the common-good world we want to live in. Without discounting the fact that there is so much still to be done, when you look at how we have dealt with issues like race, like environmental stewardship, like health and longevity, and even the drop in violent crime, you will see that our progress is due to so much more than the laws that we have enacted.

We need to talk about something beside and beyond the political system. We need to address how our institutions will work together and thrive rather than merely survive.

Indeed, it's worth looking at it this way: Instead of just wielding laws against each other, wouldn't it be better if we made accountability more of an integrated part of our culture? I've oftentimes defined culture as "what we do when we're not being told what to do." And there's another world that describes culture: habit. And *habits* exist in *habitats*.

And we actually have been enormously successful in regulating our world in this manner. Really. We just aren't used to thinking about it that way.

Egg on Their Faces

What do eggs and cars have in common? They both relate to the complex world of regulation.

Let's start with cars. It appears that automakers are voluntarily engaging in more recalls these days. That's not surprising, given the drubbing that Toyota took in 2009 and 2010. A carmaker that for decades had a reputation of building cars so trouble-free that it was accused of taking the "emotion" out of their automobiles, Toyota was faced with increasing evidence that its products weren't just malfunctioning — they were killing people in the process. Toyota started off by denying the problems, then became defensive about them, and then apologized and tried to fix the problems *after* regulators and an angry public left the company no other choice. Not very clueful. Toyota has since had to face the fact that it can't just build better cars — it has to rebuild a once-valuable brand. A lot of trust that Toyota had built up for decades instantly vaporized. Too bad. For decades, it had a nearly unblemished reputation.

Other car manufacturers took notice, identifying safety issues and "outing" themselves — recalling their products before the regulators and the public even has a chance to get itchy. Good for them, and good for us! Cars are complex machines, and even though they are more reliable and safer than ever, they are not perfect. We shouldn't expect perfection; we should expect vigilance and a constantly improving attention to these matters from the manufacturers. That very attitude and sense of action is what should be predictable and accounted for. We should applaud this new era of *pre-regulated cluefulness*, and ask for more.

On to eggs. Some half-billion of these little protein packages were recalled throughout the United States in 2010 due to salmonella contamination. But over in Britain, which faced a similar situation a number of years ago, the cases of this type of food poisoning are becoming history. Why? Because U.K. farmers started vaccinating their chickens, which can pass the salmonella virus into their eggs. This isn't breaking news. Since the late 1990s, the cases of salmonella poisoning from British eggs has dropped some 90 percent. The U.S. Food and Drug Administration doesn't require this practice, an added step that would add approximately one cent for every dozen eggs. That the FDA doesn't require this may be a pity, but the issue is — and should be — bigger than a federal agency.

There were a lot of bad eggs out there in 2010, but they aren't coming from everywhere. In fact, it appears that most of the eggs came from a producer with a history of health and labor violations. Unfortunately, the national story put egg on the faces of all of those who operate in the industry. Today, when you can shop for white eggs, brown eggs, eggs that are organic, eggs that come from cage-free chickens, eggs that come from free-range chickens, and even eggs that have boosted levels of Omega-3 fatty acids, wouldn't it be a value-added component to market eggs as having come from vaccinated hens? There's probably a host of political reasons why our federal food safety agency hasn't been able to effectively regulate this situation. But that's not really the point: I want some pre-regulated eggs in my omelet, and I shouldn't have to wait for a law to be passed or a regulator to come down heavily on an egg producer.

There are lots of ways that legal regulation can help us, but there are also ways that we, in concert with the providers of the products and services that furnish our lives, can create regulation just in our choices and in being clueful to what we're being offered. So, thank you, automakers, for not having to wait until the National Highway Traffic Safety Administration and an angry public get involved. Thanks for being clued in to how you can gain the trust of your customers.

Now, how about a little pre-regulation from egg producers? Anyone want to sell me eggs from chickens that have been immunized? I promise you that I'll happily pay more than another penny for a dozen.

Taking the Loophole out of Regulations

There are no loopholes when we regulate by culture. Here's my favorite twenty-first century regulation. It's part of Flickr's posting policy page:

Don't be creepy. You know the guy. Don't be that guy.

This regulation says some very important things. It says that you're smart enough to know what creepy is, right? And it also tacitly says that I'm not going to police you. Your best friend is.

It's not like we're likely to ever stop needing the tool of regulation by laws, rules, and regulations. There is great power and efficiency to regulating that way. There are things that we need to rigidly understand in black and white. However, our regulatory needs around things like morals and ethics and other qualitative, but truly important items, which seem to be in the news a lot these days, aren't being very well met by regulating by law alone.

Perhaps we should revisit that word "and" again. In addition to our legal tools, let's see what it's like when we add a little cultural regulation at something like ethics. That seems to be an area where being policed by having to look at our best friends in the eye could produce better outcomes.

Truth vs. Truthful

A Matter of Habit(at)

THE CIVIL RIGHTS ACT OF 1964 WAS a landmark piece of legislation that set in law the equal rights that African Americans had been promised after the Civil War. And for a short period after that most tragic period of American history, they did have them, at least in part. In the early days of Reconstruction in the late 1860s, African Americans were elected to state legislatures all across the South; Freedmen's Bureaus were set up to assist former slaves' transition into free citizens; the Thirteenth and Fourteenth Amendments erased the dreadful stains that had marred the U.S. Constitution for seven decades. African Americans were no longer three-fifths human, nor chattel possessions that free states had to return to their owners should they escape to their jurisdictions. (Those who worship the "original intent" of the Constitution might want to keep those original slave clauses in mind, don't you think?)

But laws giveth, and laws taketh away. Certainly the terrorism of the "first" Ku Klux Klan in the 1860s and 1870s did much to steal away the former slaves' short-lived freedom. But politics and politicians also played a major role in that tragedy. As Northern politicians, primarily members of the Democratic Party, found it advantageous to ally themselves with Southern whites (Southern black officeholders were almost all members of the party of Lincoln), they turned a blind eye to the Jim Crow laws that retuned most Southern states to something close to how they operated before that blood-soaked war between the states. Perhaps the culmination of this was the 1896 Supreme Court decision *Plessy v. Ferguson*, which enshrined in law the ironic concept of "separate but equal" and allowed for all those "whites only" drinking fountains, schools, swimming pools, and other public amenities.

The Civil Rights Act and the laws and regulations that grew out of it were powerful, and remain so. They represent some of the great triumphs in America's history. They were produced through political struggles in the U.S. Capitol. But those laws would not have been passed if it weren't for what occurred outside that temple, during the years of struggle and the suffering that African Americans, led by powerful figures like Martin Luther King, Jr., Fannie Lou Hamer, Bayard Rustin, and innumerable others, marched for their rights in cities like Selma and Birmingham. Rabbis, nuns, white Protestant clergy, and idealistic Northern students also encouraged the laws' passage, and "ordinary" people like the martyred Michigan house-wife Viola Liuzzo who came to march with them. These brave souls certainly weren't spectators of the common good — they were actors.

At that, however, those landmark pieces of legislation did not instantly change the culture and magically create racial toleration. Racism continued (and continues) to plague African American citizens. It wasn't enough — it isn't enough — to change the laws. Minds must change as well. Laws and government can help make that change. But no matter how good, how powerful the law, it is never enough. If widespread change is to be gained, it is through a larger force: culture.

Again, one way we can define culture is *what we do when we're not being told what to do.* It is a fluid unity of our habits and our habitats. Looking at race relations, we look at the laws associated with the Civil Rights Act, as well as the legislation rooted in them — municipal fair housing laws, equal access to government services, and the late-1960s War on Poverty. But we also augmented these laws by building a culture around them.

On television, there was *All in the Family*'s Archie Bunker, who allowed us to laugh at bigotry. There was the world of *Sesame Street* (which never even used the words racial relations), which taught me as a child — and has taught my children — the joy of people of all colors and ethnic backgrounds sharing the same neighborhood. In popular music, "crossover" producers like Berry Gordy, Jr., and Phil Spector opened innumerable white kids' ears and minds to black music and culture.

 But no matter how good, how powerful the law, it is never enough. If widespread change is to be gained, it is through a larger force: culture.

It doesn't diminish the great accomplishments of Jackie Robinson, Rosa Parks, and Julian Bond to say that Sly and the Family Stone and the Jackson Five carried on their work in a profound way. They did so by redesigning our culture.

Regardless of how well you think he has done as president, the election of Barack Obama was, to put it mildly, a very big deal. But that historic election was not made possible just because the law allowed it. It occurred because our culture created whole generations of people who thought that having a black president was not a big deal. *Of course,* we can have a black president — and one whose mother was a remarkable white woman from Kansas whose given first name was Stanley. We went from "not" to "why not?"

In other words, we integrated a value, a desired common-good outcome into our culture. And that created a more powerful foothold in our society for the values of racial equality and integration than just passing laws, essential as those laws were and continue to be.

Are racial relations "fixed" in this country? Hardly. All you have to do is peek behind the curtain of our prison system to understand that. The point is that racism is not just a problem — it is also a dilemma. It would behoove us to understand that no matter how far we've come, we still have miles to travel. Yet, while we must never forget that we still have far to go, we should always understand that we have also made great progress. We have found imaginative, empathetic ways to talk and interact around an extremely difficult issue for this country. (And not just for this country, as racial tensions throughout the world can attest to.) And that progress, past, present, and to come, is and will be the product of both laws *and* culture.

We're on a similar journey of creating a culturally-regulated habitat with environmental sustainability. Clean air and clean water are essential to our world's health, and thus our own. We certainly have seen a lot of legislative activities aimed at that outcome. But environmental sustainability also is the perfect example of an issue that isn't very well treated under a legalistic framework.

First of all, just to look within our borders, it's very difficult to get environmental legislation passed. The relative unity of Democrats and Republicans that allowed "green" laws to pass in the '60s and '70s has all but evaporated. Part of that is due to the fact that those laws, and the environmental consciousness associated with them, have been remarkably successful. Our lakes and rivers are, generally speaking, much cleaner than they were a half-century ago. More and more cities and companies have recycling programs. Businesses have

habit(at)

arisen that harvest for profit the rare earths and other valuable materials from discarded electronic equipment. Large sections of the Northeast have been reforested. We've raised a generation of people who are demanding that the goods and services they purchase have sustainability integrated into them, by design.

As with race relations, we certainly have further to go. In the Midwest, agricultural runoff remains a legitimate concern as many communities experience pollution in their water supplies. Strip mining of coal has resulted in environmental degradation in large swaths of Appalachia. Energy production in Louisiana and Texas has ruined acres of wildlife habitat. But let's be clear: Someone isn't waking up in the morning and thinking, "Gee, what can I do to hurt the environment today?" It is happening because of other design as well: Society has other needs, some of which can conflict with environmental goals — food and energy, most notably. The politicization of green makes any further legislative progress toward building a more sustainable society more difficult than it has been in the past. Look at all the sound and fury leveled both for and against cap-and-trade legislation, for instance.

There's something else that makes it difficult to address these issues solely through legislation. Environmental threats transcend political borders and are thus out of the reach of a nation's environmental laws. China burns innumerable tons of soft coal, long considered an environmental evil in the West because of the high level of greenhouse gases it emits. Much of the smog that Chinese power and manufacturing plants emit floats into the atmosphere of other nations. Los Angeles can't regulate against the particulates and gases generated in Guangdong. The Kyoto protocols, the 2010 Copenhagen Climate Change Conference, and the guidelines established in the United Nations have all been noble efforts, but they've actually achieved little, at least so far. Even those nations that have signed onto the Kyoto protocols, such as Canada, don't always adhere to them.

Again, I'm not saying that we shouldn't have environmental laws and regulations. I am saying: They're not enough and because of that perhaps we're putting too much emphasis on that approach. What's more, with government finances becoming more and more tightly stretched and budget deficits unlikely to disappear any time soon, regulatory agencies simply won't have the resources to enforce these regulations as vigilantly as the laws require. If we want to live in a greener world, it is also up to us as active citizens to be stewards of our surroundings.

So, how do we achieve that? Should we all stop driving cars? I suppose we could all disconnect from the power grid and heat our houses with wood. Practical? Not in the least. (For one thing, how long would our forests last under such a regime?) Grow our own organic food? We can do some of that, but that wouldn't be enough to feed everyone even though organic food has become more and more available on most of our supermarket shelves.

And that points to our best opportunities for making a greener world. We can make use of a tool nearly all of us have — namely, our purchasing power — while becoming more mindful of the things we buy. The opportunity is right there in your pocket: use our dollars to reward companies whose products and services reflect our values, and withhold them from those that don't. Instead of buying a gas-guzzler, we can buy a Toyota Prius or a Volkswagen Jetta with a diesel engine. And look what's happening because of that: the Mercedes S Class — the ultimate plutocrat's mode of transportation — now offers a model with a hybrid engine. As I've noted, we're raising a generation of people demanding that the goods and services they purchase have sustainability as an integrated design. And in our market economy, that is a much more powerful force than governmental regulation.

If you go to a meeting and ask who's ticked off about cap-and-trade legislation, you'd probably get half the crowd angered about it occurring and the other half upset that it isn't happening fast enough. But you won't get many people enraged by a Chevy Tahoe with a hybrid engine. Vehicles like this are an example of how we go about regulating our world in terms of an outcome by integrating the design and the common good. And remember, tools are impermanent, so these vehicles represent merely the beginning of what will come later.

There are purists who bewail, for instance, the fact that Wal-Mart and Target are putting more organic produce on their shelves, along with other sustainability initiatives. But why is this a problem? In some environmentalist circles, there is a mentality that big is bad and that small is inherently good. But that perspective isn't necessarily true. A small farmer trucking in her vegetables from the country to an urban farmers' market is a less efficient user of energy than a big retailer that can transport organic food cross-country via rail. If we truly want to remove environmentally damaging pesticides from our farmlands, then we'll need to do it more broadly across our communities and our culture. And large-scale retailing is a very powerful tool if you want to leverage the buying power of our communities. If we really want the positive outcomes of that type of food design, organics shouldn't remain expensive boutique items.

 We're raising a generation of people demanding that the goods and services they purchase have sustainability as an integrated design. That is a much more powerful force than governmental regulation.

The purist mentality also robs us of taking a good idea — eating more organic food and thus putting less pesticides and herbicides into the soil — and scaling it for widespread use. Or take transportation. Wouldn't it be preferable to change General Motors into a big green machine, rather than have it disappear, along with thousands of jobs? The fact is, green is becoming good business and it is we, the buying public, that have made it that way. To flip 1950s General Motors president Charles Wilson's famous pronouncement: What's good for America is good for GM. More and more companies are getting the message — not by regulation, but by more and more people insisting on green products. That's a pretty nice way to make a healthier environment, and it produces far less anger. And, not unimportantly, more commerce.

Beyond a Sick Care System

Another Naked Eight attribute that we're not as far along in our cultural redesign efforts is health and wellness. If we're creative about it, and we are certainly starting to design that way, we can look forward to great cultural habitats here as well. These days, health care isn't primarily about health. Mostly, it's about sick care. Despite some of the arguments made during the 2010 "debate" over health care reform legislation, there are very few places in the world where you'd rather be sick than in the United States. The quality of sick care in the U.S. is, generally speaking, superb (though not everyone has easy access to it). The problem is, we're sick a lot. Our current culture has a consequence of producing a lot of negative health conditions, as well as what health care providers call co-morbidities — one or more illnesses present at the same time in the same patient, such as type two diabetes and congestive heart failure. This is responsible for a huge percentage of our country's skyrocketing health care costs.

In other words, we have designed a "culture" where we tell ourselves that it doesn't matter how badly you eat or how little you exercise — we'll fix you, either through surgery or medication. We've designed a world that doesn't require a lot of physical movement. Typically, the food that's often cheapest to buy (and certainly the easiest to prepare) is fatty, salty, and heavily processed. And thanks in large part to the abundant subsidies we shower upon corn growers and sugar beet farmers, we've created a society with more access to calories than ever before. In fact, that was exactly the intent behind this cultural design, which dates back to World War II: Produce as many calories for as many people as we could in as short a time frame as possible. It was an effective design for a nation sending millions off to war. And it worked! But then, the war ended. And the food design we created for it did not.

The Second World War ended over half a century ago and we are left with the design's unintended consequences. Now we're fighting a different war: a war against obesity. In food deserts — urban neighborhoods and rural areas where it's nearly impossible to buy healthful food without traveling great distances — high-calorie food is just about the only form of "nutrition" you can get. But like the energy example above, it's not fair to think that folks working at your local fast food restaurant wake up every day and say, "Gee, let's get to work on creating a public health epidemic." Again, many of our designs are unintended — or at the very least, their consequences are.

Quite frankly, it doesn't matter whether the consequences were intended or not. What's most important is that we need to redesign — to reverse-engineer our way out of the current design, which has created a habitat that is just not sustainable.

In health care, our approach right now is to subsidize access to the sick-care system, rather than engineering and designing a habitat that is built around the Naked Eight value of health. We can redesign in a number of ways, some of which we've already touched upon. We could create building designs that encourage us to move — and make it fun to do so. For instance, the stairways in our buildings can be made more architecturally inviting, so that people are encouraged to at least take the stairs partway to their destination.

We need to redesign — to reverse-engineer our way out of the current design, which has created a habitat that is just not sustainable.

And there are numerous other creative possibilities as well. We could use digital technology to help us interact around activity more easily. There already are apps that allow us to measure how many calories we're burning when we engage in certain exercise activities, and can show us over time how our heart rates and blood pressures are improving. There are designers who are exploring the "gamification" of health care, developing applications for smartphones that can "reward" physical activity and otherwise make exercise more fun. (Some companies are participating in "Biggest Loser" types of competitions to see how much weight their employees can take off — those who lose the most become the biggest winners.) Several IT developers are working on software for handheld devices that can help patients with chronic conditions better manage their diabetes, Crohn's disease, or other chronic conditions through diet and medication reminders.

But that's just on the symptom side. We also could develop handheld technology that would guide you through the supermarket, not just to the best deals (which aren't always the best dietary choices), but also to the healthiest food, perhaps with the incentive of a coupon or two. We could create games for smartphones in partnership with the *Eat This, Not That!* books. If I'm hankering for a bag of potato chips, I could shake my iPhone and it would say, "Have you tried roasted green beans? Or the new Popchips products, a healthier snack that's neither fried nor baked, but is just as crispy?" (Popchips is an example of a great snack food design. Here's a huge shout-out to those folks in San Francisco!)

In sum, we have designed ourselves into sick care. Now we need to design our way into a health and wellness society that would allow us to rely less on that care. It's not just cheaper; it's more enjoyable to be healthy, yes? A perspective like this would allow us to construct a common-good community where the Naked Eight attributes are integrated into a holistic design. And it would bring us — indeed it already is bringing us — new designs and profit-making businesses.

I used the word regulation at the beginning of this chapter, but regulation, in essence, is about purposing *all* of our tools, our technologies, and our institutions toward the betterment of our communities. But the more we think about regulation merely as laws, the more we will frustrate ourselves. Our common-good outcomes will be held hostage to the Outrage Industry — or at best, will be left with half a promise just as the post-Civil War laws did. It takes a lot of redesign to create a culture that truly honors our common-good Naked Eight values.

Regulation, in essence, is about purposing all of our tools, our technologies, and our institutions toward the betterment of our communities.

With that in mind, let's take a look at the ways we can redesign — and have designed — for the emerging post-political world. By post-political, I mean that we can still honor our political traditions, whether you are a Democrat, Republican, independent, or any other political (or apolitical) stripe, but we don't have to be permanently shackled by these political dogmas. Our political perspectives can be useful for how we initially approach and frame an issue. But taken too far, they limit how we think about an issue, whom we allow ourselves to think with, and most importantly, how we can design better approaches. Designing better communities and a better world — and they *do* go together — is more possible than ever. And that's because of the new global habitat that is emerging: a *networked* world.

What Would Superman Do?

(He'd save America. He's done it before.)

In June 2011, the U.S. Supreme Court overturned a California law banning violent video game sales to minors. It was a difficult decision to come to. Undeniably strong arguments were made from all points of the spectrum, and there were pairings of justices who rarely side with each other. If you read the arguments, the opinion, the concurrence, and the dissent, you will see that intelligent people on both sides made solid, yet conflicted points. This is about more than violent content. It concerns more than the ironic ability to make it illegal to show a minor a naked breast of a woman, but perfectly legal to depict her being murdered. And it involves more than the difference between violence left to the imagination, like a novel, and immersive violence made possible in a video game. This issue is bigger than the First Amendment and how it applies to minors. It's about the current state of our culture and the inability to regulate it — indeed the undesirability of regulating it — with a blunt instrument like a law.

In their thoughtful and enjoyable book, *Freakonomics*, Steven Levitt and Stephen Dubner wrote a chapter on how Superman took out the KKK. In the 1920s and 1930s (and again in the 1950s in the American South), membership in this racist group was strong and building. And our Constitution's protection of Freedom of Assembly rightfully prevented laws that outlawed the Klan — right up until they committed violence. Regardless of the fact that nearly everyone concerned knew that these assemblies were exactly the issue that led to those deplorable violent acts, the right of everyone to convene with whomever, whenever is sacrosanct under the law of our land.

So, what did Superman do that was beyond the power of the U.S. Constitution to accomplish? He made the Ku Klux Klan look *stupid*. Kids who read his enormously popular comic book adventures and viewed the 1950s TV series saw hooded Klan members depicted as idiots holding un-American views — unintelligent miscreants who did not understand that the United States of America stood for justice and liberty for all. Superman's heroic powers were wielded as a cultural tool, so that kids everywhere could find the superhero in themselves. And American superheroes aren't racists, by the way.

As is often the case, fathers want to be seen as superheroes in the eyes of their children as well. For many of those dads, it became increasingly uncomfortable to risk having their kids find their Klan robes and hoods in the back of the closet. Sure, it might not have been illegal to have that robe, but who needs a law if your kid thinks you're an embarrassment?

Did Superman get rid of the Klan outright? Of course not. But he did make significant and positive strides where the law alone could not.

Back to the video game issue. Feeding our kids a steady diet of realistic violence undoubtedly desensitizes them to violence of all types. You really don't need much expert testimony to understand that. Ultimately, that desensitization view permeates our culture as children become adults.

But in order to effectively put to rest a challenge such as this one, there needs to be more than a simple ban. When we have a cultural challenge, we need a cultural fix. What if we took the approach that gratuitous violence produced for purely entertaining purposes, especially when it is produced in a way that is intentionally designed to be attractive to children, just isn't *cool*? All it takes is for all of us to stop supporting that type of product through the most powerful tool at our disposal: our cultural taste. If our store shelves were stocked with video games that showed acts of *overt* racism and misogyny, would there even be a question regarding the cultural outcry that would occur?

What if we all found a little bit of superhero in ourselves and did our part to rid our virtual streets of violence when it's beyond the capabilities of our cops, courts, and jails? Isn't that what superheroes are for?

Green Just Got Greener

What's better than a nicely designed machine? A green one, naturally. Ford was well-advised to team up with SunPower, the Armani of solar panels, to create the newest and greenest idea of them all: a solar-power generation system for the home to balance the amount of energy it takes to recharge a car like the Ford Focus Electric. Once these green-loving minds merged, the idea came to fruition that SunPower would sell this device to Ford Focus Electric buyers, very smartly making the Focus Electric the greenest electric car on the market as of 2011.

The system essentially provides the home with the same amount of energy it takes to charge the electric car, based on an estimated average of miles driven per month. By means of solar panels and lots of sun, this new generation system cancels out all energy consumed by the already eco-friendly car, thus making the driver a saint of the streets.

And the shiny red bow on top of this green marvel? After throwing down some $10,000 to be the greenest person on the block, SunPower will supply you with an app to control your system while you're away. Though it might seem excessive, it is a great design for the eco-conscious and one giant leap for Ford.

And you thought that a killer sound system was the coolest option!

NETWORK: The Real Killer App

L AWS AND OTHER FORMS OF government regulation are part and parcel of a command-and-control social process. And the structure of that process is hierarchy. We've had over ten millennia of experience with command-and-control institutions: from chiefs and royalty at the top through nobles, merchants, tradesmen, and commoners. The United States, of course, was designed as an egalitarian republic, without royals and nobles. But merchants and tradesmen, and even politicians, largely took their place, leaving the hierarchical structure largely unchanged. (No need to mention the slave economy of the cotton fields and rice paddies of the South.) You can easily identify these organizational designs by the existence of tools, such as titles. Whether it is in government, business, the military, churches, or academia, titles have been a hallmark of our world and they serve as roadmaps as to how someone fits within their organization, where he or she is in the pecking order.

Hierarchy developed because our economic system has been rooted in extracting economic goods out of or off of the ground, whether those goods are crops, animals, petroleum, or metals — in other words, "things" that then became the basis of all transactions. Hierarchy makes such transactional systems function most efficiently. Even in the industrial age, which dislodged feudal aristocrats from their long-held roosts, captains of industry still used command-and-control to keep their great masses of workers functioning as part of the machinery of production. In our post-industrial age, hierarchy still functions as the main engine of economic efficiency.

But more recently, in addition to that — again, the key word is AND — we have something else: a new overlay of networks. Very simply, a network is an interconnected group of individuals who influence one another. Networks are relational, not transactional. And while power can be forced down a hierarchical command-and-control structure, power can't be asserted in a network, because people self-select themselves into that structure. They can leave when it suits them. These networks work best when they're constructed around qualitative properties, like ideas and values, such as the Naked Eight attributes, for instance.

In a network, there still are those who wield more influence than others, but here those influencers are more likely to be engaged in questioning, debate, and (just as important) *listening* than a hierarchical leader would be. Debating an influencer is far less likely to result in the questioner being jailed, fired, or fired upon by the leader's police force. But more than that, influencers *earn* their position, rather than asserting it with a form of power or control. They earn it by engaging in activities that build trust. They are *collaborative* — its members co-labor; they work together.

Hierarchy = (Trans)action
Network = (Inter)action

To be sure, networks aren't a new phenomenon. Medieval guilds were networks of craftsmen who provided mutual support, standards of conduct, and group identity. More recently, ethnic groups emigrating to the United States formed networks that offered their members access to employment and housing, spiritual and financial support, shared memories of their home countries, and in many cases, services such as insurance, banking, and burials. Many were centered around a parish or neighborhood. As ethnic ties loosened among those immigrants' children and grandchildren, new networks arose — many still associated with churches and synagogues, but many others around professional and civic service organizations like the Jaycees, Rotary, Lions, and dozens more. These organized kinds of networks still exist, of course, though in many parts of the country, they have diminished.

What makes today's networked world distinct from those older networks? The networked world has arisen in part because in many municipalities, these ethnic and club ties have frayed over the last few decades, as detailed in books such as Robert Putnam's *Bowling Alone* and *Habits of the Heart* by Robert Bellah, Richard Madsen, William Sullivan, Ann Swidler, and Steven Tipton. Those older networks were typically hierarchical, with leaders and followers. They also tended to be less self-selecting — if you were a Polish Catholic, you belonged to the Polish Roman Catholic Union, and were less likely to be accepted by the Knights of Columbus or the Hibernian Order. And as I noted, you also could argue that the prosperity of post-World War II consumer capitalism made us less connected to our communities and more to our own individual and family lifestyles. We don't feel we need that same level of social support, at least outside of a therapist's office.

Yet, we still hunger for social connection. And thanks to the astonishing capabilities of digital devices and wireless technology, our ability to connect has never been easier. But these connections are different from most of those bound by "older" types of networks. Do social media represent the "new" Lions and Shriners? For many of us, they do. The key word here is *mobility*. We no longer are tethered to a centralized communications system. Daily newspapers no longer bind together our municipalities as they used to — we're less and less on the same page, so to speak.

 The networked world is not as much about authorities as those who have authoritative voices as deemed by others.

That can mean that we are susceptible to less reliable information. But at the same time, the information we do receive is less top-down — we can learn important news through networked links. With the decline of centralized communication comes the capability, *if we so choose*, of interacting more deeply with our communities — to be active citizens, rather than passive consumers of information and commerce.

The networked world is not as much about authorities as those who have authoritative voices as deemed by others. In the networked world, your reputation and your ability to influence are as valuable, if not more so, than your direct headcount. Indeed, your indirect, self-selected headcount is the true measure of wealth in a network. The strength and quality of your connections are more important than their number. In other words:

So, where do you and your common-good values fit into this networked world? Just about anywhere you want to be. All it takes is your common-good intent and your increasingly easy ability to join others who share your goals and your values. As recent global events have shown us, there literally isn't a political jurisdiction that can effectively shut your connectivity down. In other words, if you want to design yourself into meaningful action, there has never, *ever* been a better time to do so than now.

The networked world is not defined just by experts, it also is defined by those who have expertise and that expertise need not require a graduate degree — or any degree at all. It does require providing a distinctive knowledge or capability that your network trusts. You can post a video on YouTube and get a million viewers, and no one asks you what film school you attended. Fifty years ago, you'd have gone to your doctor, and he — back then, he would nearly have always been a he — would say, "All right, this is what's wrong with you and this is what you're going to do." A couple of decades later, the conversation would have gone something like this: "All right, this is what is wrong with you and this is what you're going to do. And if you'd like, you can get a second opinion." Now, before you've even called for an appointment, you've been on WebMD.com, you've seen the Lipitor ads, and you go to your doctor and tell her what *you* think is going on with you, and ask if she would confirm it and assist you in the treatment.

The networked world is not a utopia. As I've noted, we also can use networks to wall ourselves away in gated communities of influence and information where we communicate only with those who share our opinions and cultural prejudices. Or we can use technology as a way to keep from engaging with *anyone* directly — as Sherry Turkle observes in her recent book, *Alone Together* — digital technology and social media "make it easy to communicate when we wish and to disengage at will." Texting and posting can keep us from having to actually spend time with anyone face to face, where most meaningful relationships still take place.

 The networked world is not defined just by experts, it is also is defined by those who have expertise and that expertise need not require a graduate degree — or any degree at all.

Stephen Downes, a Canadian researcher and thinker, specializing in the intersection of education and digital technology, who

It's not the people you can count.
It's the people you can count _on_.

frequently writes about the idea of "connective knowledge" —
describes influence as a function of four properties:

1. **Diversity:** A person who communicates with a diverse audience will be more influential than a person who communicates with a uniform audience.

2. **Autonomy:** A person who is free to speak his or her own
   mind, and is not merely parroting some "official view," will
   have more influence.

3. **Openness:** A person who writes in multiple languages, or who
   can be read on multiple platforms, or who is not limited to a
   single communications channel, will have more influence.

4. **Connectivity:** A person you can communicate with, and who
   will listen to your point of view, will have more influence
   than a person who does not.

Angertainers and most advocacy groups vigorously discourage
these multiple networked interconnections. Very simply, interconnections are a threat to them. It's hard to sell black and white to groups
that embrace a spectrum of colors. Ultimately, the Angertainment
and advocacy industries really are hierarchy-focused, however
"rebellious" and contrarian they may want to appear. A hierarchical
network is made of a solid fabric, like a security blanket; a modern-day
network can have a looser weave, with spaces that let in light and air.

The key point here is that a networked world is one that is *open
to interconnection* between its constituents. We are open to influence
from the "outside," and able to influence others. This doesn't mean
that we cease to be Republican or Democrat, conservative or liberal,

or Jewish, Muslim, Christian, Hindu, agnostic, or atheist. But it does mean that we are not solely those identities; we have the opportunity to communicate — to be in a common place, in many common places. This is part and parcel with what British futurist and business strategist Josephine Green calls "democratizing the future" — designing a world where hierarchy doesn't disappear, but where it becomes increasingly influenced by the common good and the ideas and needs of those at the "bottom of the pyramid."

 A networked world is one that is open to interconnection between its constituents. We are open to influence from the "outside," and able to influence others.

It's a different way of building a common-good community from what most of us know. And it requires us to think very differently about how we approach public policy, how we look at business and purchasing products, and particularly, how we think and interact with those with whom we are not in agreement. It will require us to bend, to realize that our views and political commitments can't be forced upon others — they would resist, as would we.

Earning Influence in Addition to Asserting Power

The networked world allows for what I call *influence design*. These structures, where individuals link and connect *because they choose to,* are just not places where power can effectively be asserted despite some of the desperate attempts we see on the evening news. True power in a network lies in the hands of those who wield the most influence and that may not have anything to do with their title. Just like hierarchies are designed, so are networks, and as such, influence design is a practice that intentionally creates the opportunity to earn someone's interest, rather than merely asserting what you offer. But we have to understand something all but forgotten in the Age of Angertainment: For this mutual influencing to be successful, we will need to be intentional, be open to others' views and activities, and create new common-good designs in those gray areas that exist between the poles of black and white.

Some recent examples of this can be seen in the amazing changes (done with amazing rapidity) during the Arab Spring. The same can be said about how rapidly voices assembled to produce enormous pressure on Congress to stop recent legislative proposals regulating intellectual property protections on the Internet. In all these cases, people who are not the type, whom you would commonly call "powerful," were able to join forces and successfully stand up to those who thought they had the power to assert their views and control. Why is that? One reason is that large hierarchical organizations usually have enormous wealth in the form of finance and sometimes property. But networked organizations also have important forms of wealth in terms of human capital and oftentimes, in the form of moral authority. Another reason is that these people were linked by a common value that turned into a common desire for change; their moral authority was more powerful than the "authorities." And finally, is the fact that throughout these networked initiatives were people who were able to create the conditions of influence through a mix of technologies and their ability to articulate a magnet-like story that people wanted to become part of. Their tools? Empathy, excitement, and a deep sense of purpose linked to common values. These mostly nameless players were supreme influence designers, indeed.

Yet, as I hope to show you, influence design makes perfect sense for the world that is evolving all around us. It also makes perfect sense if we look upon the common good, not as a political football, but as something that is truly *common* to all of us.

So, while power players might still have the ability to command and control their organizations, they should also consider augmenting those activities with an active "listen and respond" interaction with the networks that they exist within, whether those networks consist of the community at large, their customers, their parishioners, their citizens, or even their own employees.

This is not a dreamy notion. It not only can *work* — as I have shown you with just those couple of examples — it already is.

From Strategic Inefficiency to Breakthrough Relationships

Institutions celebrate efficiency around transactions, such as selling products or services. Making a deal effectively — that is, in a timely manner and with the greatest financial gain — is the outcome of acting efficiently. It means making all the right moves at the right times, and having all the right answers to clients' questions.

When it comes to relationships, however, we shouldn't be so linear. A relationship is about sharing values and morals; it's an *interaction*, not a *transaction*. While being efficient is a useful business skill to possess, I think that in order to build great relationships, sustainable relationships that go beyond a mere single transaction, we need to be more strategically inefficient.

Let me explain. The more you and your coworkers, bosses, and clients know about one another, the easier it will be to land that transaction. When we know more than one thing about each other, we allow ourselves for more areas of possible connection. And the more connections we are able to construct between each other, the less vulnerable we are to a single disagreement. Our relationships become more sustainable, and it will have more tensile strength. Listen, we'll always disagree at times, and it's important that we do. But by knowing each other well and finding things out about one another by small, strategic inefficiencies, we will be able to disagree without being *disagreeable*.

Transactional relationships may be about the lowest price, but premium interactional relationships are defined by the greatest value.

Strategic inefficiency could mean grabbing a coffee with a coworker and instead of discussing work, jumping into a discussion about something deeper, like your companion's distaste for working in teams or passion for political debates. It could mean killing some time on the Internet, searching things that interest you, which can lead you to a discussion board and introduce you to a stranger with common values and goals.

We are so in love with technology, all so interconnected through the Web, that I think spending a little time enjoying our journeys both on and off line could lead us to solid, breakthrough relationships and ultimately, to premium transactions where you are differentiated from the crowd for something other than that you're the cheapest deal. Transactional relationships may be about the lowest price, but premium interactional relationships are defined by the greatest value.

(Y)our Opportunity to Influence:
The Seven C's

INFLUENCE DESIGN IS NOT A SYSTEM. It's a framework — a way of thinking. Transactions require systems and hierarchies. Interactions are rooted primarily on mutual trust. Reputations are earned — not asserted.

In a networked world, it is virtually impossible to control people; but as I said in the last chapter, you can influence them based on trust. If people in a network don't trust you, your reputation — which can be defined, in part, as a capability for influence — will be minimal. That's true whether you're a citizen or a group that seeks to build a common-good community, or a business that wishes to engage buyers of your product or service. And if you want to earn influence, you must do so intentionally. Your common-good goals and how you seek to achieve them must be designed and communicated in ways that are built to be properly understood. In other words, while you cannot assert and control how influential you are, you most certainly create the conditions to earn it.

 Reputations are earned — not asserted.

For instance, those on both the right and the left who see government and business as adversaries may have a difficult time understanding one of the key tenets of influence design — namely, that business and government are (or should be) collaborative builders of common-good communities, though they use different tools. And the connection point is the community — specifically, that the citizens and customers who make up that community are actually one and the same. In a networked world, we can easily walk around with multiple identities, multiple definitions of who we are and who we associate with. Our opportunity is to act as participants in building that common good, regardless of which particular hat we are wearing at the moment.

Our networked world is a very large marketplace, comprising spaces where we trade goods, services, and ideas. But in this busy world, products and services are usually a commodity. How people "feel" about offerings in the marketplace is where the premium lies; a bit later on, we'll revisit that in terms of a business's "Social Relevance." Briefly put, social relevance is the next step beyond social responsibility. Why? Because if you're not responsible, you shouldn't be in business in the first place, and increasingly, the influence of networked people will ensure that. Why again? Because if you are responsible, it really shouldn't be enough to separate you in the marketplace either. Being responsible has become table stakes; it's what allows you to enter the marketplace, but it certainly is no guarantee of success. "Hi, I'm responsible!" doesn't sound so sexy, right? But, "I'm more relevant to you than the next guy" actually does make sense in a networked world where success depends on your

(Act)ive

ability to be influential. As always, the quality of the product or service must be excellent, of course; but beyond the transaction around the "thing," the interaction, what the thing "means" must also bring increased value ... best yet, a value derived by aligning with common good values.

 Social relevance is the next step beyond social responsibility.

We've been sold a false debate between those who espouse the ideas of the economist Milton Friedman, "Business is in the business of making money, period," and those who say that businesses must "give back" to society. Business, after all, isn't simply "in the business of making money" (at least, an honest business isn't). It is producing something, a good or service, employing people, paying taxes, etc. True, businesses are seeking to make a profit because without it, they will be out of business. But increasingly, the way a business differentiates itself in today's busy marketplace comes through its actions and its ability to speak to the common-good interests and values of its employees, its customers, and the community at large. Go beyond a shareholder focus and into the world of stakeholders and you will find that there are many, sometimes counterintuitive, folks who are very interested in your activities. And interacting transparently and honestly around the Naked Eight attributes of a healthy community is a great way of building trust, differentiating your offerings, and enrolling as many of those people into your success as possible. So, business is still in the business of making money and designing products and services that speak to people's values are increasingly the way to do it. No more argument! This is an important tactic that works well beyond the business sector, by the way.

I'll use Loomstate as a nice example here. Created by the social innovation geniuses Rogan Gregory and Scott Mackinley Hahn, Loomstate has successfully woven together fantastic designs, easy on the earth environmental processes, cutting edge educational mentorship for tomorrow's fashionista creators, and have wrapped it up in a price point that doesn't break the bank. They are a relevant and successful venture under just about any definition.

Businesses that go above and beyond the expected should be met with a consumer who's ready to go beyond the expected as well. In other words, use the power of your network beyond the power of your dollar.

So, what's your role in supporting businesses that design values into their goods? Seems kind of obvious, right? Give them your business of course. But that's so twentieth century in its thinking. How about giving them your business *and* the power of your influence? Like any other kind of business, these socially-relevant players want to make a profit. Profit drives economic growth. And that's a good thing. But profit derived from producing other social benefits beyond the simple transaction, not only drives economic growth, but greater social impacts as well. And that's a very, *very* good thing. Today, businesses that go above and beyond the expected should be met with a consumer who's ready to go beyond the expected as well. In other words, use the power of your network beyond the power of your dollar.

Here's one of my favorite illustrations of this point. My friend Eve Blossom runs a company called Lulan. Eve travels the mountains of Southeast Asia and finds grandmothers who are teaching their granddaughters the art of silk weaving. She gathers her weavers into cooperatives and sells museum-quality silks here in the United States. Eve also has begun to branch out into producing organic cotton textiles. She takes a significant percentage of her profits and puts them back into those villages in the forms of money, food, and health care. Very nice.

Lulan is run as a self-sustaining, profit-making enterprise, as well as one producing textiles whose components are environmentally sustainable. But that's just the start of it because Lulan is also about something much bigger and important. In fact, it is *so* much more than just a weaving cooperative. Eve, who is an architect by training, didn't enter the silk business solely because of the product, but also because of the process. She wanted to do something that would keep young Asian girls out of the brothels of Bangkok. Many girls end up there because their families are so poor that there are no other opportunities for them.

It's not that there aren't laws against that kind of exploitation. But for a whole host of reasons, those laws are rarely if ever enforced. Since the laws are not an effective tool against human trafficking, Eve has moved upstream. She is using the market power of people desiring beautiful fabrics to affect the same common-good goal. Given the politics of many countries, her non-political approach is much more effective. That's because the people who purchase Lulan's beautiful pillows have *participated* in Eve's work — by purchasing the pillows and telling their friends about the beautiful story behind those pillows. They aren't just buying a "thing." They are buying into the social relevance underlying the item. Sure, you can buy a pretty pillow at the mall, but can yours keep a little girl from being sold into the sex trade? Eve's textiles have deeply meaningful common-good attributes and outcomes designed into the product and that is what makes her goods much more than a commodity. They have a story — a common-good story. And those who purchase a Lulan pillow become characters in that story, and thus a part of that story's character.

And then, there's a small, but fast growing, shoe company, named Oliberté. Each shoe is made with handpicked free-range leather. The rubber soles are natural, and much of the process is done by hand, stitching included. But that's just the design of the value(s)

shoe — the "thing" you're buying. Now listen to the behind-the-scenes design. All of the manufacturing occurs in a variety of African countries that have distressed economies. Around 50 percent of its workforce is comprised of women. The company provides job security, free lunches, tea breaks, and maternity leave. And, remember, all of this takes place in some of the poorest communities on our planet.

Perhaps you'd like to give someone a gift of a pair of shoes. Oliberté can take you an important step forward — from giving the gift of shoes to also giving the gift of a job, a purpose, and a paycheck. With locally-sourced materials and a devotion to being faithful to the environment (it even has a shoe-recycling program), perhaps the most important of all of Oliberté's efforts is its intention to wean these poor nations from a dependency on aid and assist in transitioning the economies in to more vibrant and stable forms of self-sufficiency.

Or consider organic food. There's an argument that we might be better off if we were to buy organically-grown produce and free-range chickens, and so on, right? There are those who'd like to pass laws forbidding farmers to raise anything but organic food products. But such laws wouldn't even get a committee hearing. So, what's the real-world, common-good option? Buy organic food yourself, without a law insisting upon it, and then influence others to do so, too. And guess what also happens? You ultimately will have much easier access to these products as the marketplace grows. And more often than not, over time, the price will go down as well. Nice, huh?

Ready to Wield Some Common Good Influence?

As individuals, we have never had more ability to design and build the world we want to live in — again, because of networks. So, how can you design your influence to make it effective and constructive? I call the framework for doing so the "Seven C's."

1. ***Calm down.*** Don't respond to what's "wrong" through anger and adversarialism with the "other side." To have influence, particularly with those outside your networks, you need to engage in trade. That is, engage in conversation, which means both talking and listening.

   We all know what listening is, don't we? Nope, sorry. Mostly, we don't. Listening requires patience while someone else talks, even when that person is long-winded or indirect or somewhat inarticulate or rambling down the trails of various tangents. It also means considering the possibility that the person you're listening to — especially if that person holds very different views than you do — might actually be right, at least about some things, and that you might be wrong, at least about some things. In other words, listening means being open to the idea that you might have to change your mind and let go of some of your most treasured opinions.

   What's more, conversations typically don't create results — not within an efficient time frame, at any rate. This is a journey; common-good change takes time. You're planting seeds, and the fruits won't instantly appear. Patience and an understanding that better is perfect are essential. It's good to think of yourself as a student, because usually what you'll find is that products and services are being offered in their current form for some rational reason (even if it's to keep costs low, rather than to improve the products' quality). While that doesn't mean that there aren't ways that you can suggest to improve the item, it does mean that learning a bit about its current design will help you as you get into your productive conversations with businesses and (potential) customers.

2. ***Be a connoisseur.*** Pick an issue, a practice, or a product that you'd like to influence. If you want to be a civic designer, pick

something that really engages you — something that really holds your attention, entertains you, and makes you think that you want to get to know more about it. The Web has plenty of information to help. Want to get the skinny on all things organic food? Check out localharvest.org. Interested in the latest and greatest on what your t-shirt can do for the world? Head to your handy Web search bar and type in "sustainable clothing resources." You may be surprised by how many sources of resources there are. These are but a couple of examples, and of course be mindful that not all of what you find is 100 percent reliable, but with the help of other people in your network — and interconnecting with other networks — you'll have the ability to get a sense of, not only what great services and products are out there, but also the great people behind them. Remember that you're not in the *commodity* influence business now; you're also trading with great people engaged in great common-good efforts, not simply buying their products.

3. *Curate* the information and sort through what is helpful and what isn't. This might lead you to discover different approaches to achieving a common-good improvement in what interests you. Curation isn't just finding what's good. It is distinguishing the truly excellent from the good. Remember, you don't have to be an expert. You will have grown valuable expertise through your focused exploration and that is exactly what will make you an influencer in the future. All those nuggets of information that you're gleaning along the way will serve as the ammunition you'll be using later on as you become an authoritative influencer.

4. *Coproduce.* Again, being a consumer is inherently passive — we just buy what's there. We typically don't know how our purchases are produced. We forget that our hamburger came from a cow because it's square and wrapped in plastic or sits inside of a bun.

But if we are connoisseurs, if we are actively seeking to learn more, we can take advantages of opportunities to contact producers of goods and services and do so in productive ways that say, "Make this, and make it in this better way, and I'll buy it and tell others. If not, I won't." When we become engaged in commerce ourselves, we become traders. (And, to use another metaphor interwoven throughout this book, we become weavers of the common good.) Your values won't be integrated into goods and services you want if you keep those values secret. Don't keep companies that want to earn your influence in the dark. They will surely value your input if you practice the first step: Calm down. Why? Because when you've put anger aside, you can present yourself as important (and free) research and development for the people producing goods and services. Put out helpful, positive energy, and you will almost surely receive the same back.

Now, I know that this sounds pretty intimidating when you consider yourself as one lonely voice out there in the wilderness. But remember that it's highly unlikely that you're alone in your feelings and you have absolutely the most powerful connecting tools ever concocted in human history. Start searching the blogs, start asking some questions, and start gathering your tribe.

That is exactly the genesis of many of the non-governmental organizations that are partnering with manufacturers as they go about producing goods that meet the increased labor and environmental standards that we are demanding of them. These NGOs in some important ways are co-producing the products that you and I find valuable because they are there working to ensure that what we're buying actually meets our values.

5.   *Compensate.* Put value behind what speaks to your values. Compensate the producer by purchasing it. But that's just the start. As I just mentioned, helping the producer make the product or service better is another form of compensation. But one of your greatest opportunities in a networked world is that you can and should compensate a business by mobilizing your network on his or her behalf as well. Get those with whom you are connected to buy the product or service. There's little that will be appreciated more than enlisting yourself as part of their sales force, as the authentication that comes from your word of mouth is worth much more than their paid advertising.

6.   *Be conspicuous.* In other words, don't hide your capacity for positive influence. It used to be that conspicuous implied conspicuous consumption: "Look at me! I'm rich and famous and drive a Ferrari, and you can't." The rich and the famous are still supreme influencers in our world, of course. But in the networked world, influencers don't need to be rich or famous. But they do need to be knowledgeable connoisseurs, as I've described. And they need to be willing to show what they've learned: "I'm driving a hybrid, or supporting this local restaurant, or buying these particular jeans, and here's why. So, how about you?"

7. ***Connect.*** Influencers cannot and must not hide their author-itative voices under a bushel. They must broadcast. And digital technology creates so many effective ways to do just that — out to their network, and beyond.

At this point, you may be shaking your head: "If only it were that easy. Even if I am an 'influencer,' my 'network' is small. It's a big world out there, dominated by large global corporations with intricate networks of global supply chains and massive marketing budgets. How can I possibly have any effect?"

Try telling that to Eve Blossom. Try telling that to green products companies like Caldrea and Method, successful upstarts in the soap and cleaning products categories. The terrific folks behind these terrific products have serious business minds. And they know their chemistry. In fact, they know their chemistry well enough to under-stand that cleaning away the dirt and germs doesn't have to equal the word toxic. Adam Lowry and Eric Ryan at Method along with Kevin Rutherford at Caldrea (which also produces the ever-fun brand, Mrs. Meyers) are making big impacts from relatively small platforms. Their successes have come, not from massive marketing budgets, but by influencers and their networks.

And big companies *are* being influenced. Partly in response to companies like Caldrea and Method, international giants like Procter and Gamble are introducing numerous "green" cleaning products. There's nothing wrong with compensating big companies for efforts like these. In fact, I'd encourage it.

Citizen responses via their networks mean that businesses also have to be more attentive to the value and values their products and services bring. This also promises enormous opportunity. In an industrialized, command-and-control economy, mass marketing was effective (mostly). Conceiving large groups of consumers as "target markets" still works, more or less. Super Bowl commercial time remains in high demand, after all, because it reaches so many people all at once, and TV spectators of the big game still seem to respond. Most likely, there probably always will be a mass market.

In the networked world, influence is no longer primarily the preserve of those at the top. It's not really bottom up, either. It's inside out. Influence can be broadcast from nearly any direction. And the networked world is growing. It is going to have a greater and greater influence on the common good, in commerce, in government, in non-profits — in just about every sector.

But that influence will only be powerfully good if those who wield it do so *mindfully* and *intentionally* — by design.

With that in mind, let's look at influence design at work. First stop: business.

But Sometimes, Political Anger Is Good; It Gets Things Moving, Right?

No doubt, there are productive uses of anger. It's a great motivator. But, man, is it a lousy steady diet. It festers, it's contagious, and while it may dislodge something that doesn't work, it's not the right energy for building anew. And really, at the end of it all, isn't building something new more important?

It's interesting how you can track that in products. Now, there are those who rail against gas guzzling SUVs and raise their middle finger at every Chevy Suburban they pass. But where does that get you? And then, take Toyota's first hybrid car, the Prius, and look at how it took positive energy (and less hydrocarbon energy for that matter) to build something new and even how it took them a couple of tries to get it right.

The first version sold just okay. Why? Because it was an interesting new engine in a same old same old car body. The second version was a statement, however. It looked different. The Prius 2.0 was a rolling political statement ... but not necessarily an angry statement. Rather, it was a positive statement about "look what my car does." But guess what? Now you're starting to see the same hybrid technology in those SUVs. And the angry people are just going to have to look forward to something else to rail against. What started out as a political statement is now being more broadly accepted without the politics. I think that's progress.

PUTTING THE Seven C's IN ACTION

Frameworks oftentimes seem a little ethereal and impractical until they're tied to something real. So, to better show how the Seven C's work (and work together), let me spin you through that lens of twenty-first century common-good consumption by using an example. In this case, let's go back to my friend Eve Blossom and her innovative business, Lulan.

Calming down:
Seeing little girls living the sad lives of sex slaves in Bangkok undoubtedly would anger you (and as a dad of two young girls, it certainly upsets *me*). Perhaps it makes you even angrier to know that there are actually laws against this practice — laws that have had little impact on this terrible situation.

That anger is good. It shows that this is something you don't want to tolerate. Still, I'd suggest that simply being angry won't do anything for those little girls; and ultimately, it won't do anything for you other than leave you with bad feelings of helplessness. Better to do as Eve has done, and transform that anger into calm, intentional purpose. And let me tell you about my friend Eve: She knows anger and she knows how to use it to motivate her. But I've never known her to wallow in it comfortably. She's too much of an actor to sit in that space and seems to always find a path to move forward into with purpose, passion, and yes, calmness. Indeed, her calmness translates to those around her as competence. Eve's calm also calms down everyone around her and it's one of the reasons that she may be one of the coolest people I've ever met.

Connoisseurship:

Take the time to understand the issue in terms of, not only what is happening, but also more importantly *why* it is happening. There are lots of ways to glean that information, but what you'll discover is that the legal system that is supposed to protect those little girls has significant challenges and some of them of a very deep-seated nature, namely corruption. Pass more laws? Not likely the best response. Dig a little deeper, and you'll start to uncover something further upstream: economic desperation that results in parents selling their children to keep food in their mouths. So, you start shopping for a non-governmental organization that works on alleviating rural poverty. They're out there, and many of them are doing an admirable job. But you may well find that they're not as focused as you really want — your anger was directed at a very specific outcome of rural poverty. So, in your digital detective work, you run into a terrific social enterprise named Lulan. You start to learn that this isn't just any weaving cooperative. It's a common-good engine and it's focused right where your heart hurts.

Curating:

Again, that NGO may be doing a good job — and there is nothing that is stopping you from contributing to their mission. But you're looking for something that's, not only doing a great job, but that is about more than giving dollars to an organization a half a world away. The very mind-set that brought you through the connoisseur exercise is what allows you to engage in the action of curation. You have understood the lay of the land: more laws, NGOs, and this innovative cooperative. Now you're ready to put your knowledge into action and make an informed choice about where to focus your dollars and attention.

Coproducing:

Now, pivot from angry spectator to purposeful participant. It's time to go out there and buy a product from Lulan. You like it because it's beautiful to the touch, to the eyes, and to your heart. It calms your anger. Perhaps you like it enough that you want to see other items produced through this social design, so you contact Eve and say something like, "I really liked that bed throw. Do you think that you could create a table runner if I got enough folks in my networks turned on to what you're doing out there?" And Eve, being the Eve I know, will probably say something like this: "Let's do it. Here's my business model. Here's how many people that we'll need to get into this run, in order to meet the mission that we both seek and for me to keep my business sustainable, which is an important consideration because we both know that child prostitution isn't going away tomorrow." Or she might even say, "How about contacting a retailer and letting them know that you would appreciate seeing products like mine on their shelves? In fact, how about getting some of your friends to do that, too?"

Compensating:

Believe it or not, you've already compensated Eve in two important ways — first, of course, by buying one of her products. She owns a business, and no one gets paid and her mission becomes mission impossible if you don't do that. You also compensated her by reaching out to her and applauding her for doing something good and being creative about it. Eve, like so many others designing in this matter, is not doing this because she is solely focused on running a profitable business; she is mission driven, and she'll most certainly appreciate hearing from others who share her passion and want to assist in this better outcome.

Conspicuousness:

So, now that you have this beautiful runner with a story underneath that is even more beautiful than the table it is draped across, it's time to help spread that story. At your next dinner party, your friend comments on this new addition to your dining room. Don't merely say, "Thank you." Say, "Thank you and tell your friend that they won't believe the story and meaning behind this ten-foot strip of fabric." Indeed, that's just the start of your storytelling journey because now you can engage in ...

Connecting:

With Twitter, Google+, and Facebook, you now have the ability to become an adjunct advertising wing of Lulan. Take a picture and post it. Tell people that this isn't just a table runner. It's an anti-child prostitution weapon. And tell your friends that your good taste is based, not just what the product is (beautiful), but what it means (stunningly cool). And guess what, my Seven C's friend? You'll come off as stunningly cool, too.

And your anger? Go use it to launch into something else.

Are You Calling for a Boycott of Irresponsible Businesses, Campaigning Against Politicians and Groups that You Disagree With?

No, more of "A seek out." Listen, there are already a lot of people out there doing the boycott thing, wielding those kinds of sticks. I don't think that I need to add my voice to that. I'd much rather be in the carrot business. Sure, punishing those who disappoint us is one way to change things, but so is reinforcing good behavior. And it strikes me that we're pretty well practiced with stick swinging and we could use some time tending to the carrots. If you were raising kids, which one would you rather emphasize? "You're a jerk and you're grounded until you have grandchildren!" or "Way to go kiddo! Let's do that again!"

Green as Hyper-conspicuous Luxury

One of the great markers of acculturated change is when a product or an idea is considered "luxury" or "trendy." Once it is connected with one of those terms, you know it has been accepted into society.

An article in the April 28, 2011, issue of *The Economist* offered a prime example of an acculturated product — the low-emission luxury yacht. While "green" has been a trend for the past few years, this is one of the first times we've seen it married with "hyper-luxury." This piece about super-luxurious green yachts — equipped with solar panels, sails, hydro turbines and more — raises the initial question: "Who could afford this?"

Then, the next thought is: "Why would anyone burn all that money, especially in our crippled economy, on a monstrous toy?"

The noteworthy part about something so out-of-this-world, like a $100 million green yacht, is that when those with the money invest in it, this technology will become more widely used. And what happens when something becomes common? The prices go down. If the mega-wealthy continue to spend their money on green technologies, they are in a very real sense putting their money toward a future in which products with the same technologies will be available for those of us that aren't exactly in the yacht market. But look at the iPod. Prices are far lower now than when the product was first introduced, and it's hardly a rare product. In fact, sometimes, it's funny to get onto a bus or enter a room and see how many people have one in their hands. Green yachts represent a higher level of technology, but one day, they might scale down to something obtainable to the commoner.

When it comes to public-policy outcomes, green voting through design is far better than not voting green at all. If the wealthy continue to put their money (and their votes) toward greener efforts, we just might see some of the green tech that makes that over-the-top yacht so cool, showing up in our weekend dinghy.

And that's worth making waves over.

Corporate Social ~~Responsibility~~ Relevance

IN THE LAST CHAPTER, I FRAMED how individuals can utilize their active participation in commerce to coproduce better common-good outcomes. And when I refer to commerce, I mean more than goods and services. The same framework applies to how you could think about whom to vote for, what school to attend, which hospital system to choose, or even which particular place of worship you'd want to attend. In this chapter, we'll focus on the production side.

I hope that this perspective will be helpful to both entrepreneurs and established businesses that want to differentiate themselves in the marketplace. I also offer these ideas to the people I addressed in the last chapter: As a coproducing customer, you'd be wise to seek out and support those organizations that attempt to design and offer items and services seeking to help build common-good influence.

And when you find them, think of ways that you can help them do even more. Production and consumption are ends of the same spectrum, so why not design from both ends and meet in the middle?

I've noted that we should all be involved in trade. Among other things, that means that we should not see business as an activity that's separate from the public sphere. It's true that too many businesspeople believe that that's the case — that their public role is simply to be a private organization that focuses on the bottom line. But that's wishful thinking. To one extent or another, most of us in our (mostly) capitalist society are involved in the business of trade. We may work for someone. We may work for ourselves, even if that entails a side project to our day jobs. We may be the parent, baking yummy cookies for the local school fund-raiser. We may be invested in the stock market with our retirement or perhaps our union is. We may offer our handmade products through online sites like Etsy or Craigslist. We may provide freelance writing or bicycle repair or website design. Most of us, in other words, have something to trade. Business is intertwined with both our public and private "selves."

Production and consumption are ends of the same spectrum, so why not design from both ends and meet in the middle?

For the most part, businesses interconnect with their communities primarily through the marketplace — through the transactional exchange of goods and services for customers' money. In Ancient Rome, a marketplace was called a forum, a word we now use to describe a place where ideas, rather than goods and services, are exchanged. The exchange of ideas also occurred in the forums of Rome. Perhaps we should again view the marketplace as a forum in both senses, i.e., what a business "sells" is, not only a product or service, but also the ideas and ideals behind it. Our networked world is requiring companies to move beyond one form of connection between themselves and their customers — *transaction* — to something deeper — *interaction.*

Perhaps we should again view the marketplace as a forum in both senses, i.e., what a business "sells" is, not only a product or service, but also the ideas and ideals behind it.

There are many reasons for this transformation of how we think of the mission of the business community and our requirement that they actively participate in creating common-good outcomes. Some of this results from an increasing inability of our government designs to successfully address all of our common-good needs. Even at that, a major reason why we are looking at business differently is because business itself looks different. The twentieth century saw explosive growth in the number and size of multinational corporations, entities that not only spanned the globe and operate beyond the political borders of any one country, but organizations that amassed tremendous wealth and influence. As a result, there is a growing sentiment that businesses need to be common-good actors because they can. The key now is to turn that conversation from, "They should because it is required of them," to "They will because they will find it in their self-interest in doing so." With opportunity comes responsibility; and in this new marketplace with that responsibility comes new opportunity.

The interaction between business and society typically falls under the term corporate social responsibility (CSR). In its first iteration, in the 1980s and 1990s, CSR was defensive in nature. This was the era when companies like Nike got caught manufacturing in factories with child labor. Rightfully concerned, Nike led the way in how to set a standard and policed itself. CSR in this iteration points to: "We weren't acting responsibly, but now we are, so how do we prove it to you?" The designs in that iteration called upon partnering with other sectors, usually the fast-growing community of non-governmental organizations (NGOs). That way, business could point to the opinion of a trusted third party to authenticate their activities. This presented a new way of thinking of regulation beyond the traditional method of producing and policing laws alone.

The next step on the CSR ladder — and it was an AND of course — was a focus on philanthropic action. As businesses became wealthier, the public increasingly expected that they would become more philanthropic and fund the activities of nonprofits. But limiting our view of CSR to this type of thinking plays into that false dichotomy we discussed earlier between "making money" and "giving back." The latter implies that companies took something that didn't belong to them to begin with. But that's usually not the case. Economic growth over the centuries bears that out. These days, society is asking more of businesses, particularly larger enterprises, and that's perfectly appropriate. But corporate response has often been a guilt-ridden one: "We have to give back because we make a profit. And the way we're going to give back is by being philanthropic — giving money or volunteer time to various causes." Again, this is a *very* good thing. All you have to do is look at Bill and Melinda Gates and understand the power behind that kind of thinking.

Undoubtedly, philanthropy is almost always a wonderful addition to our communities. And, of course, we want corporations to police themselves to common-good standards as well, whether or not they partner with NGOs to do so. But to be truly socially relevant — to *build* better communities, rather than simply *maintain* our communities, as they currently exist — companies need to integrate common-good designs *into* their products and services. They can't thrive just by being responsible; they must be more relevant than their competition.

To build market share, companies need a sense of a shared market: a forum, in other words. And as successful marketers can tell you, a key part of building market share is building mind share — getting people to think of your product not only as the best in the market, but also as a product that does some good in the world. Building that kind of mind share is how businesses can design their influence. And having that kind of influence can be extremely helpful for a company when it stumbles, something we'll discuss later in this chapter.

So, what does it mean to design the common good into your products? In the previous chapter, I mentioned cleaning product companies like Caldrea and Method. These consumer product companies engage in charitable works, to be sure. But the most powerful thing that they're doing is producing cleaning products that are designed to minimize their environmental impact. That is why they exist; it's their mission and vision. That's how they create their market share and how they coexist next to giants like Procter & Gamble. Method and Caldrea's products are intentionally designed to conform to a common-good outcome, and that design is building its influence in the marketplace. As I noted in the last chapter, Procter & Gamble *has* been influenced: It's starting to look at higher efficiency and lower environmental impact in many of its products. In fact, from toilet paper to laundry detergent, from the way their goods are packaged to the way the products are being reformulated, this consumer products giant thinks that there's big business in servicing the needs of those who desire environmental stewardship as an integrated product design. So, let's show them just how big the market is and let's make sure that we take care of the little guys like Method and Caldrea along the way, too. Please.

 A key part of building market share is building mind share — getting people to think of your product not only as the best in the market, but also as a product that does some good in the world.

Another example? Your corner organic co-op is having a great impact on great big companies like General Mills. Aside from the interesting fact that every one of their cereals has whole grains now, you also might find it notable that under their banner, you'll find organic products like Muir Glen, Cascadian Farms, and Lärabar.

What these product designers understand is that business needs to have a broader sense of what CSR is. CSR should be about listening and responding to common-good conversations. These conversations occur beyond the legislative realm, in the broader regulatory marketplace of reputation — a place where products and services can have Naked Eight attributes designed into them, rather than legislated upon them. And this mentality can create all kinds of opportunities, even for large, established businesses whose opportunities for growing market share might seem somewhat limited.

A big part of the challenge that many of these corporations face is that a small, but vocal, number of people have negative perceptions of their products — or more accurately, "parts" of their products. Take SUVs. For busy families, particularly those living in suburban areas, SUVs are an eminently practical form of personal transportation. But many perceive these vehicles, with some justification, as wasteful gas-guzzlers. The problem, however, is not the SUV in and of itself — the problem is the gasoline that goes through the SUV. If it ran on a more renewable form of fuel, it wouldn't matter as much what kind of mileage it got.

Or take soda. The high-fructose corn syrup that most sodas contain has been linked to an explosive rise in childhood obesity. Not only that, but influential food activists like Michael Pollan have argued that the corn used to make this cheap form of sweetener is having serious negative effects on rural economies and the environment, not to mention our health. But it's not the drink itself that's really the issue; it's a particular ingredient.

This is where I'd like to introduce an idea I first brought up in Chapter 6: *pre-regulation*. If regulation is nothing more than producing more accountable behavior, pre-regulation occurs when an organization (either for- or nonprofit) identifies and polices itself to that standard before it is forced to do so. In the case of soda, school districts and other government entities could ban soda in their schools; that is certainly a national trend. Soda bans reinforce a growing public perception that PepsiCo, Coca-Cola, and other manufacturers are making products that are bad for us. These companies could choose to fight this perception by creating one-way messages about their products that don't address this perception, but make us "feel good" about their products. They might tout that their plastic bottles are made partly from plant sources. Or they could simply ignore the conversation and try to wish the problem away.

 If regulation is nothing more than producing more accountable behavior, pre-regulation occurs when an organization identifies and polices itself to that standard before it is forced to do so.

Or: They could pre-regulate themselves. There are plenty of influential political advocates who wish to turn beverage companies into the next tobacco companies if they don't get their act in order. Beverage companies would be well served to understand that they're better off aligning themselves with common-good values than fighting them and losing at the end of the day. This isn't to say that these companies aren't aware of the problem — they are. But in addition to their robust advocacy activities in legislative circles, note that these beverage companies are starting to get wise by getting involved in the common-good conversation, to listen and to respond. Their opportunity is to increase their positive mind share in order to maintain or even grow their market share.

So, how might that work? Think of how Apple created a whole generation of people who will only buy Apple products because the company put those products into grade schools — first computers, and now iPads. So, perhaps Pepsi and Coca-Cola should be thinking of Aquafina and Dasani that way. Pull those high-fructose corn syrup sweetened beverages out of those schools and start putting a healthier product there instead. Start pushing flavored waters. That way, Pepsi and Coke will create a whole market for itself: a whole category that, while still relatively small, is growing faster than soda. And the company would be growing it for the right reasons — particularly, the Naked Eight attribute of health and wellness.

Ultimately, Coke and Pepsi aren't in the high-fructose syrup business. They're in the beverage business. So, one of the questions for them becomes, can they engineer that negative ingredient out of their products? Can they develop different sweeteners? Some beverage makers are touting their use of sugar instead of corn syrup. And there are other potential sweeteners, such a stevia, which is extracted from a South American leaf and which has barely any of the hypoglycemic impacts of high-fructose corn syrup. What we could have, then, is a redesigned product that could be less harmful to soda drinkers, the environment, and not unimportantly, benefit the beverage manufacturers as well.

But as a customer, you have to remember your role. It's not enough for soda companies to produce them. *You* have to buy them. It's not a successful redesign if it just sits on the shelf. Coke and Pepsi are currently trying to design values into their product. Will you give them the value, so that they can sustain the effort?

In the emerging networked world, people are becoming aware of, not only what products and services are out there, but also the greater impacts of those products and services. Increasingly, we want to align with institutions that share our values. And more and more, we're willing to pay a bit extra for it. The participatory customer says: "Before I give you a value, show me that you share my values." Value added means values added. And I'm going to demand that of a business in a lot of different ways: how it treats the employees and the environment, and how well it makes good on its promises. "I may love the look and feel of your company's T-shirts and the price is rock bottom, but they're of no real value to me if I find out they're made by enslaved children. Engineer that out of the design. Prove to me that you have integrated fair labor practices into that T-shirt. Then, your product becomes truly valuable to me." It's worth reiterating here that many of the laws in place can help prevent (or attempt to prevent) child labor, but you as a consumer have another ally out there in the form of the many NGOs and journalists that scour the globe for those unfortunate practices. Pay attention to them and let your favorite manufacturers know that you are doing just that.

The opportunity always lies in being able to differentiate yourself, and that's through design — not just how your products look and perform, but how common-good attributes are built into them.

If you're a business, you may want to be the commodity player. You may want to produce the cheapest product in your market. Good luck. Usually, there's room for one of those in every segment; in some segments, there is no position for one at all. In any case, there's no added value — no value for the community and no premium for your company. In order to compete, you'll need to provide something more — something more valuable most likely, but also something that people are actually willing to pay for. And as I noted in the last chapter, there's more than one way to "pay" for something. On the business side, the opportunity always lies in being able to differentiate yourself, and that's through design — not just how your products look and perform, but how common-good attributes are built into them.

In the networked world, businesses are less and less able to control or "push" an emotional response. They need to have a *pull* strategy, where they draw people to and enroll them into their message. And that requires creating and designing a reputation. If you, as a business, are able to create the conditions to earn a valuable reputation, you'll influence important communities into wanting to transact with you. That community could be your employees. It could be your customers. It could be your vendors. It could be regulators. It probably should be all of these. Put another way, brands that speak to the common good will be pulled along into prosperity by the community. But — and this is an important distinction — a reputation is something that can only be earned. These days, a valuable brand brings together what you say about itself and what others say about the brand (and the company behind it).

To illustrate this push and pull in action, let's look at a line of products beloved of my daughters, Tom's Shoes. What my girls love aren't just the shoes themselves, but the story behind them. Tom's Shoes have social impact designed into every pair of shoes: When you purchase a pair, the company provides a pair to a needy child in the developing world. Buy a pair of shoes; give a pair of shoes. Tom's is using their customers as part of the design.

In marketing its products, Tom's does have a push strategy, through advertising and sales efforts. But it also has a *pull* strategy — an influence strategy. The company encourages people to share their stories, and to go along with the Tom's staff and do "shoe drops" in needy communities. There's marketing push and a reputational pull. Put together, that's Tom's identity strategy, and that becomes the company's marketing strategy. Tom's has distinguished itself in the crowded world of shoe marketers because of that design.

A key aspect of a pull strategy is *listening*. Pushing a message goes in one direction, from business to customer. This is what we traditionally think of when we talk of business marketing. Pull goes both ways. If I'm a business, I need to come to you, my potential customer, with a product or service that shows that I've been listening to you. You say that you want clean clothes, but don't want

Relevance +
Responsiveness
= Value

phosphates in the river. I respond by producing a laundry detergent that gets your clothes clean without phosphates, and I make certain that you know exactly why I've designed it this way. And as a business, my hope is that you'll respond by saying, "You listened to me. You were listening to something beyond the transaction. You wanted to interact with me, and I will compensate you." The compensation may be that you pay me more money. Or, if you're an employee, your compensation may be to say, "I'll work for you for less money, or I'll work longer hours or I will be loyally employed by you for more years." And above all, in our networked world, that compensation can be: "I'm going to tell a friend about you."

Regulation is nothing more than being held accountable to a common-good standard, regardless of whether that standard was written in law or defined by your company's reputation within a community or communities.

But there's more that influence design — incorporating the common good into a company's products — can do for you. Let's revisit pre-regulation and what that can mean. Here, I'll address businesses directly, but customers may wish to listen as well, because they are a crucial part of this conversation.

When issues are discussed that involve your company or your industry sector, it's worth understanding that you will be regulated in some way. Again, regulation is nothing more than being held accountable to a common-good standard, regardless of whether that standard was written in law or defined by your company's reputation within a community or communities.

With regulation, especially the legalistic type, my experience shows that your business typically has three options: try to kill the regulation; attempt to get yourself grandfathered out of it; or get invited to the table to write it. And I can assure you that option three is a great one. But only, and I mean only, if you're *invited* to the table. One of my pet sayings is that it's better to be at the table than on the menu. But in order to be invited, you have to earn your place there. Pushing your way in, especially by asserting yourself as having the authority to craft legislation, is dangerous — many will question your self-interest and motivation. Being invited publicly, on the other hand, is a great position to be in.

There's a wonderful additional benefit to being seen as a pre-regulated organization, by the way. And that is this fact: Everybody has a bad day. And on that day, you will have a choice: You can look stupid, or you can look evil. Guess which one is the wiser choice? Stupid, of course. You can apologize for being stupid; that shows that you can learn and change your ways. And generally, the public is very forgiving of someone who says, "I'm a good organization that had a bad day. Please forgive me." Evil, on the other hand, is a very deep hole to dig out of.

But here's the thing: You can't claim stupid on day one. You have to have built the reputational capital beforehand — prior to your crisis — because in addition to an apology and contrition, you will need to show that your organization was good in the first place — that you were producing common-good behavior when no one was looking. If you want to influence the outcome of your bad day, then the path begins by integrating common-good designs into your daily activities and production. Starting now.

Here's an example of pre-regulation from my experience as an officer at Target. In 2005, friends in the law enforcement community informed us that bad guys were stealing cold medicine products containing pseudoephedrine off of Target's shelves and cooking them into methamphetamine. At first, we connected with pharmaceutical manufacturers to see whether they could produce an effective cold medication that didn't contain pseudoephedrine — in other words, to see if product redesign was possible. Unfortunately, it wasn't.

So, instead, Target performed its own redesign — in this case, it redesigned its vending practices. It moved all of the products containing pseudoephedrine behind the pharmacy counter. It also worked with law enforcement agencies and the community to create other regulatory activities around the purchase of pseudoephedrine. Target communicated the intention of wanting people to understand why it was doing what it was doing, and why it was important to the company *and* the community. By doing so, Target didn't just change their actions; it changed the conversation. That way, the young mother with a sniffling toddler in her arms would know that the reason she was being slightly inconvenienced was because her favorite retailer was taking an important stand in designing the safety of her neighborhood — which, of course, spoke to her values.

Social Entrepreneurism and Social Enterprise is the Innovation of the Twenty-first Century

Before closing this chapter, we should talk a little about a growing movement very much in line with the vision of influence design. Social entrepreneurism and social enterprise are two of the more common names that this movement has been given. It's a movement that has almost as many forms as it has names. Very broadly and incompletely, this movement seeks to align common-good goals with the self-sufficiency, scalability, and financial and managerial rigor of a well-run business. Social enterprises can take many forms; they're usually nonprofits, but they need not be. Like any other service or manufacturing endeavor, they typically have "investors" — often individuals, sometimes government entities, but also other businesses — that aren't interested in simply writing checks. They want to see measurable results in the communities these enterprises serve. Investors usually participate in the running of these enterprises, as advisors, board members, even as executives.

There are numerous examples of social enterprises that are operating successfully in the developing world. They include well-known entities that provide microfinance loans to poor people seeking to start their own businesses. Other social enterprises are producing and supplying water-purification systems and anti-malarial nets in Africa and elsewhere. Some provide meals for the poor, but also run catering businesses on the side, like the Pine Street Inn in Boston.

In my hometown of Minneapolis, a noteworthy example of a social enterprise is Baby's Space. Founded in 1998 by child psychologist Terrie Rose, Baby's Space is a nonprofit whose mission is to improve early-childhood outcomes among poor families. But it's not only the common-good mission that makes Baby's Space a superb example of a social enterprise. It's not interested in serving the role of a traditional charity, simply helping poor families survive. It wants them to thrive, to improve their situations. Both families and the nonprofit are collaborative, active participants in Baby's Space services of creating models for high quality, high impact childcare built from the baby's perspective. What's more, Baby's Space is working to become self-sustaining: It owns intellectual property that it can sell to other nonprofits that wish to emulate its model elsewhere in the country.

And here's another one that I just love. The animal shelter in Aspen, Colorado is a for-profit business that supports its animal welfare mission by offering services, such as grooming and boarding privately owned pets. And through its shelter, you can get a dog for a day if you'd like. Instead of being penned up, this shelter's dogs are often out on mountain hikes with visiting families. This past year, my family had a wonderful day hiking in the woods with a beagle named Genevieve, and it really enriched our experience as well as hers. So, what we have here is an outfit that has changed the conversation and design from merely housing animals that have no home to an animal service and welfare business that provides a wonderful quality of life for all the animals it encounters. And, I should mention: They're very profitable. Wonderful!

In short, social enterprises represent a worthy and innovative design approach to the challenges facing our world. It's a growing segment that deserves your attention, your business, and your influence upon and through your networks.

The fact is that we need organizations of all types and all sizes to participate in the forums of interconnection and exchange, in order to build common-good communities. This requires us to design spaces where these kinds of exchange can take place. These places cannot be adversarial in their design, as is the case of the various political Temples of Conflict. What we're talking about here is alignment — a key element of influence design.

And in order to do that, these diverse interests are going to need new kinds of gathering places where they can understand each other as complementary pieces in a common-good whole, rather than competing adversaries over the community purse.

Why All This Focus on Business?

Well, one reason is that there are a number of businesses that have become bigger, wealthier, and more powerful than many governments on the planet. They're that important in our lives and as such, we should focus on them. We've seen the rise of empires, kingdoms, religions, and nations. And multinational businesses are the newest institutional form to have that kind of global dominance. I find it interesting how we talk about business needing to fit into society. That's a common statement, right? But what's funnier is that we don't talk about that in regards to other institutions in our society. We talk about how government, science, and a religion fit into our lives, but not how it fits into our society. But Business is treated differently. Perhaps it's because it's the newest kid on the block to assume that kind of societal impact and power?

Sometimes, the Best Gift Is to Allow Someone to Make One for You

There is an interesting, but ultimately disturbing trend in our mind-set around consumption. With examples of over consumption obviously present around us, there is an understandable and important discussion to be had around that dilemma. There are voices reacting to this with the call to drastically reduce our consumption, and while there is more than a little kernel of truth to that attitude, taken too far, it's easy to see how damaging that call can actually be.

Again, I can understand how this might be appealing to some. But there's a problem with this too-simple solution for decreasing consumption. What this mind-set seems to overlook is that when we aren't consuming, we aren't producing. And when people aren't producing, people are left without jobs. How's that for holiday spirit?

To illustrate through a related issue, I've said in the past that if we were using renewable fuel, we wouldn't really care what kind of mileage your SUV got. I think it might be useful to look at consumption in a similar manner. To the point: It's good to make things, it's good to transport things, it's good to vend things, and it's good to buy things. These are all activities that allow people to be productive and compensated. But perhaps the more critical issue is how much of those myriad of activities involve the extraction of things that are finite.

Listen, I know that it's not going to be possible in the short run to run our consumption off a totally renewable platform. But there are some interesting models to look at, such as William McDonough & Michael Braungart's provocative school of thought around the concept of cradle to cradle. www.mcdonough.com/cradle_to_cradle.htm. Imagine a world where your bio plastic do-dad can be easily and cheaply turned into another bio plastic do-dad. It's not science fiction ... it's starting to happen and it may just point to a whole new era of consumerism.

There's hardly an issue of importance out there that doesn't run into conflicting values and it's generally a dangerous path to solely focus on one value at the total expense of another. I'm afraid that putting a halt on consuming newly-manufactured products would result in some pretty steep issues, like more joblessness. So, here's a perspective to consider: Buy things. Support the economy. Provide jobs. Consumerism is still important because production is still important.

The question is what are you consuming?

Public Spaces, Public Places

WHEN THE VARIOUS INTERESTS that make up our communities come together in diversity, it is usually under a capitol dome or the roof of another level of government. This is not unimportant activity in the least. But we do need to constantly recognize an important thing that I've reiterated over and over: These places are designed for adversarialism. Again, it's a design that works admirably when the issue at hand is an actual policy, and where the scenario involves horse-trading between two different, often opposing sides.

But as I've also noted, too often the issue at hand is not policy, but a word that is frequently and purposefully confused with policy. That word is politics; and politics has gotten increasingly partisan in this Sudden Illumination Syndrome age. But if we recognize this situation, not as a hopeless dilemma, but as a design challenge, then we can create a new design — not a design to replace our capitols, but a design to serve as an alternative as to where we meet and how. In this case, it's building opportunities for interests to act in alignment, rather than as adversaries.

These forums, these spaces, must be purposely designed if they are to succeed, because it doesn't seem very likely that we're going to work together by accident.

So, let's return to the idea of a forum. A forum, as a market of both trade and ideas, is a place of abundance. In order to build a common-good community, we need forums where people can come together to meet, haggle, and come to a deal. This is as true in deciding a course of public action to address common-good dilemmas around the Naked Eight as it is in transacting in goods and services. In a common-good forum, we can gather to discuss, argue, and come to consensus; people can influence and be influenced. Just as economic activity can create abundance, so can an exchange of ideas. That is, as long as everyone is willing to trade.

These forums, these spaces, must be purposely designed if they are to succeed, because it doesn't seem very likely that we're going to work together by accident. There must be an intention, and that intention is to build a common-good result. These spaces should be places of mutual respect and listening, rather than adversarial battlegrounds.

To use another metaphor, we should think of these meeting places, which can be both face-to-face and virtual, as workshops where we can come together to determine our designs and figure out, together, which set of tools work best for the job at hand. The term I use for this kind of work is *consortium design*. And a design consortium is based on abundance, rather than scarcity.

Scarcity: 1 versus 1 = 1 (a survivor)
Abundance: 1+1=3 (mutual benefit)

Aside from showing you once again how "creative" (read: slow) I can be with math, these equations demonstrate the difference between a common-space design and — well, call it an anti-common space. Anti-common spaces are designs based on scarcity. In order to win, the other side has to lose. The equation in an anti-common space is 1 *versus* 1 = 1. That's one of the problems of town halls, for instance: Many are nothing more than bitch sessions, where the professionally pissed off show up and too often dominate.

In the common spaces created by consortium design, the equation is 1 + 1 = 3. Meaning: You can't do this on your own, and I can't do this on my own. But together, we can accomplish what we can't do alone.

A common-good forum design requires collaboration. And it requires people to be willing to admit that their most cherished beliefs might be wrong, or at least not completely right. But more importantly, it takes the realization that your interest is not enough to produce the entire result. In other words, this design requires participants to have empathy and respect for each other and realize that they actually need one another. Yes, we actually need each other.

Consortium design and abundance thinking require a different understanding of what influence is. It's not about controlling a discussion. It's about helping to shape it in a direction that leads to a new approach to facing a dilemma, in order to improve a situation, and thus a community. And it requires that all participants focus on at least one of the Naked Eight attributes. It requires a stance of curiosity, the ability to learn from others, and the understanding that no one does well when the community doesn't do well. The intention is to come together for generative thinking, not adversarial thinking. Everyone can have influence, but that influence must be earned. The would-be influencer needs to build trust with the others in the group. And that requires being honest and open, rather than domineering.

The chief elements needed for an abundance-design consortium to work are *diversity* and *inclusiveness*. Think of it like this: I want to build you a watch. I know that we'll need some hands, a face, gears, housing, and a strap to keep it on your wrist. Each individual element has an intrinsic value in and of itself. But it is only when we bring them all together — inclusively — that all these parts can actually produce a useful result: namely, to tell time. The same thing occurs in constructing approaches to the Naked Eight: A diversity of tools is necessary, but only when they are combined inclusively do they actually move us forward.

At this point, let me discuss a specific case where a consortium space was designed for abundance, in order to build a common-good solution. The Naked Eight attribute that this case focuses on in particular is, once again, public safety: an area where we really and truly need each other.

Fifteen years ago, Minneapolis was having a problem with petty crime — particularly shoplifting and aggressive panhandling. The problem was particularly prevalent in the city's downtown core. What's more, the press at this time was going through one of its periods of spotlighting urban crime. This increased the public perception that the problem was getting worse, even if the data showed that it actually wasn't. In any case, the problem certainly wasn't getting better. More and more business and community leaders worried that this perception would hurt the city's image, and the strength of its retail base.

Much of the concern was around the tools being used. People didn't think they were working. Some blamed the police for a lack of enforcement; others blamed the court system for not giving repeat offenders stronger sentences; still others blamed advocates for the homeless for making it difficult to get certain known recidivists who were causing crimes to be taken off the streets. There was a diversity of opinion and perception, and these opinions and perceptions weren't necessarily wrong. But they were incomplete. And as long as people clung to their particular views and the tools that they'd built around them, there would be no way to address the dilemma and improve the community.

All of this occurred before Target Corporation, my employer, had sold its Dayton's department store division. Target had its headquarters in the central city, and its flagship Dayton's store was there as well. Being a company that understood that the health of its hometown was essential to its own continued prosperity, Target was greatly concerned about the perception of downtown. As a business, it was also worried about petty thievery in its stores.

Bob Ulrich, Target's CEO at the time, decided that the current state of affairs was intolerable, and it was no one person or group's job to improve it. The entire community needed to take this on. Though there was plenty of disparate discussion and argument about the topic, what Target chose to do was host a meeting. Bob asked me and Target's Vice President of Assets Protection, Brad Brekke, to assemble a group that included law enforcement, city officials, the school district, homeless advocates, community representatives, and local businesses. Brad and I then gathered them together to meet and to talk. The chief topics we asked this consortium to address were: What did the city need to do to make its citizens feel safer? And who was making them feel unsafe? The group did have this fact in hand: 10 percent of the criminals were committing 20 percent of the crimes — and eating up 40 percent of the criminal justice budget. Ouch.

Again, the idea was to intentionally design a different kind of meeting space. So, one of the first "design" ideas that Brad and I introduced was having Target play the role of host. In other words, we didn't present ourselves as the angriest guys about our community's dilemma. Perhaps most importantly, we didn't present ourselves as the smartest guys in town, either. What we did is simply call the question. We gathered influential and impactful members of the community and set the stage: "We are all concerned, we all want basically the same outcome, and that outcome absolutely will not happen unless we all have a role and help each other out."

The next step in this new design was to listen to everyone as individuals, not as representatives of particular interests. After all, there was no one player at fault; and no one can be expected to come up with the whole fix. It's stunning to me how infrequently we engage in this important step; and I am always astonished by how enjoyable this process is. If you allow yourself the opportunity to just sit back and listen, you'll be surprised, not only by what you learn from people's stories, but also how listening to them can lead you to connections that you would have never thought of. That is the beauty of a diverse group: You get a much bigger picture of challenge and thus much more opportunity to engage in broader-based redesign.

Something that the group quickly discovered was that if they were to constructively address the dilemma of crime, they had to work together. So, its members started creating processes and technologies to share information and resources in order to keep tabs on the recidivists — the 10 percent who were causing so much strife. The approach would be very much boots-on-the-ground: storeowner calling storeowner, letting each other know, "This guy's on the street, he's been stealing from me, watch out."

Ultimately, the larger group began to think of this work as a business improvement effort. It challenged itself to offer more services, to keep things cleaner, and to establish and fund "ambassadors" on the street. The ambassadors' role was to provide a kind of additional policing. More importantly, they were there to make people feel welcome and safe simply by their presence. These ambassadors still walk the streets of downtown Minneapolis. Recognizable by their green vests, they greet passersby, pick up trash, provide directions, and offer other kinds of help to both visitors and residents.

That is the beauty of a diverse group: You get a much bigger picture of challenge and thus much more opportunity to engage in broader-based redesign.

It's not as if there weren't plenty of security personnel in downtown Minneapolis. For every policeman or policewoman on the street, there were several private security guards. But there was a major problem here: Police and security guards didn't share an inclusive culture. They didn't talk with each other; sometimes, they didn't even seem to respect each other. There are probably a number of reasons for this, but mostly it was because they had never really had much of an opportunity to get to know each other beyond their titles. By getting them to talk on neutral ground, the consortium was able to lower these cultural barriers and get both sides to see themselves as working together for a common-good purpose.

The consortium also decided to address the issue from the perspective of how retailers handle crime. Many retailers design their asset protection strategy around the design of catching and stopping shoplifters. That's one design. But that approach never satisfied my friend and colleague Brad Brekke, a former FBI agent, who is both wicked smart and a truly good guy. So, working a whole host of other community-minded actors in Minneapolis, we all agreed on forging a path that honored that intent: a consortium of diverse interests working inclusively to creatively address the conditions in the community, so that it could produce fewer shoplifters — in other words, a better habitat.

In assembling this consortium, we all designed the conversation, the action, and the influence strategy with the public at large as well as with the law enforcement community. It was all pursued with an intention of doing something for the common good and having key people understand what we were doing and why it was important to them. In other words, Target helped create a space for fruitful discussion, constructive criticism, a little venting, but most of all for collaborative connection. But at its core, it wasn't so much a formal space as an attitude. And that attitude was not that we were unhappy customers of our public institutions, but rather, we were all co-owners of the cooperative that would create a better outcome for all. The group shared technologies and designed a common culture from the components of their distinct strengths and capabilities.

These days, the streets of Minneapolis are now not just perceived as safer — they actually *are* safer. And it simply couldn't have happened solely within the walls of a capitol or city hall.

What did Target get out of this? How was the company compensated for its participation? For one thing, its community brand was enhanced. Target made new relationships that bore fruit further down the line. Its employment brand was enhanced, not only in the pride of employees who know what kind of outfit they work for, but that their quality of life at the company's downtown headquarters was made safer and better as well.

That's just one Naked Eight example of a consortium design, and just one example of how Target continually looks for creative ways of investing in the health of its communities. The fact of the matter is that when *everyone* is at the table, we can think of ways that we can play a different role. And in that totality, we then make huge strides toward making *our* communities more successful.

Here's another example of common-good forum design. Like the downtown Minneapolis anti-crime consortium, such forums typically have a specific goal — or they should, if they are to be successful. The Midtown Community Works Coalition is made of a true motley crew of interests: federal, state, and county and city governments, as well as businesses big and small, neighborhood activists, and nongovernmental organizations. Also at the table are metropolitan-area government representatives — the Twin Cities are joined by Portland, Oregon, as one of those rare communities that also are overseen by a regional entity.

The coalition came together to bring about the transformation of an old, unused rail bed running through south Minneapolis into a greenway thoroughfare that would accommodate bicyclists and walkers. It took several years to achieve, many of which involved the engagement of many parties, not all of whom originally embraced the idea. The rail bed had been constructed below street level, and ran through some of the more challenged neighborhoods of the city. Many worried that a trail running through what was in effect a long ravine would become filled with trash, or would put riders and walkers in danger.

 When everyone is at the table, we can think of ways that we can play a different role. We then make huge strides toward making our communities more successful.

But the coalition persevered, and the first portion of the Midtown Greenway opened in 2000 to great local fanfare. It is now one of Minneapolis's most treasured amenities. It's really more than a recreational trail. It has become something of an "expressway" for bicycle commuters, and one of the driving forces (pardon the ironic pun) behind the city's thriving two-wheel culture, which has become nationally recognized. That culture has stimulated numerous small businesses, including bike-frame design firms, metal fabricators, bicycle-clothing designers, and Dero Industries, one of the country's most creative fabricators of bike racks. Allina Health, one of the country's largest health care systems, courageously planted its flag in the neighborhood by locating its headquarters in a restored historic building that sits on the Greenway.

Not all common-good spaces need to be physical and face-to-face. For instance, there's the Global Dialogue Center (www.global-dialoguecenter.com), organized and overseen by Debbi Kennedy. This is a virtual meeting space where people leading common-good organizations from around the world can meet, share ideas about what has worked and what hasn't for their particular groups, and help each other come up with new solutions to their various dilemmas. Everyday, there are seminar offerings, coaching, and connection. It is just like you would if you could do it down the block, but of course that doesn't work when the person you want to connect with lives half way around the world. The idea here, again, is inclusiveness; those "outside" your network, and those interconnected with it, are both essential to abundance thinking. And Global Dialogue Center has designed away a significant barrier by removing the geographic distance we have between one another.

 Not all common-good spaces need to be physical and face-to-face.

In my home state of Minnesota, there's the estimable Citizens League (www.citizensleague.org), which for more than half a century has been creating common ground for the common good and helping create citizen-designed approaches to complex issues. If you've heard of a charter school, now you know where it was invented. In Wellesley, Massachusetts, Babson College, which for nearly twenty years has been ranked the nation's number-one business school for entrepreneurs, has an amazing soul named Cheryl Kiser. She's created the UnCommon Table: a space that is designed so that diverse interests can learn from each other and create business opportunities around some of the most complex and vexing challenges facing our communities. One innovative example is the Food Solutions Laboratory, nicknamed Food Sol and run by Rachel Greenberger (www.babson.edu/Academics/centers/the-lewis-institute/Pages/food-sol.aspx). Food Sol seeks profitable approaches to nutrition, environment, supply chains, wages, and working conditions, to name just a few of the issues that surround that most basic of human needs.

There are a couple of reasons an environment like Food Sol is worth noting. The first is acknowledging the need for multilateral, multi-sector approaches to making headway around complex challenges. The UnCommon Table methodology encourages people of diverse backgrounds to come together in alignment around common goals. The second reason is that all of this is taking place at a *business school.* That means that diverse players come together to work out solutions that also make money. And here's why that should be *very* important to you: If I regulate you into doing the right thing by law and being the smart person that you are, you will find a loophole. If I ask you to do the right thing for philanthropic reasons and being the good-hearted person that you are, you'll do it, but can we sustain your actions long-term? But if we find a way for you to do the right thing and make money doing it, and being the clever person you are, you'll find a whole host of ways to do that and more. Now that's a good result!

Want to see how we're going to design better environmental health for the world's oceans? Check out the Savannah Ocean Exchange (www.savannahoceanexchange.org) where they stage awards for entrepreneurs who bring cutting-edge environmental designs aimed at our aquatic environments. On top of merely convening interests, they've created competitions and prizes for those who want to create and sell into the marketplace around the precepts of transportation, trade, and sustainability.

And as evidence that we can innovate around our political culture, there's a group called No Labels (www.nolabels.org). This group seeks to create common ground between Republicans and Democrats, so that members of Congress can engage in principled compromise. Hundred of thousands of your neighbors have joined this group and they're making headway on important issues like the nation's budget, education policy, and trade posture. As I've said before, these folks get harassed and worse for engaging in this important and courageous work of joining hands across the political divide. These policy makers need your support and No Labels is a design with just that intention.

The unifying idea in all of these efforts is this: Our polarized and adversarial culture did not come about by accident — and building out of it won't happen by accident, either.

The Partnering Initiative in the United Kingdom is another organizing tool that practices abundance. Its website, thepartner-inginitiative.org, states, "We believe that cross-sector partnering is an important mechanism for addressing critical sustainable development issues such as health, youth employments, social inclusion, post-conflict resolution, enterprise development, and environmental diversity." The Partnering Initiative presents a wide range of Naked Eight issues and creates the space that brings the necessary diversity of interests together, so that they can be woven together.

The unifying idea in all of these efforts is this: Our polarized and adversarial culture did not come about by accident — and building out of it won't happen by accident, either. In so many cases, as I've noted, what we have are good people who are forced to act badly because of a bad design. We don't get common-good outcomes because we actually punish people within these designs for thinking collaboratively. They're forced to think of their own interests first and foremost. The alternative of acting in common, in alignment, will happen only by design as well. Sometimes, those designs will be physical places. Sometimes, they will require entirely new institutional forms.

But mostly, they will require a new way of thinking — a way of thinking that will ask of us where we really want to be spending our time and money: on war, or on trade?

Are You a Republican or a Democrat?

My Republican friends think I'm a Democrat and my Democrat friends think I'm a Republican and I love it just that way. Actually, I'm violently moderate in my politics and independent to the core. I've met too many good people with great ideas on all sides of the political spectrum to limit myself to one political flavor. And besides, my brand of politics is merely one element of how I think about how to go about making our communities better. I can look at things from the perspective of D vs. R, but I can also look at it through the prism of business, labor, environment, academia, health, etc.

Think about health for a minute. There's no Republican or Democrat "way" of being healthy. There may be political perspectives as to how you think about the tools that we've created to address the dilemma of creating better health, but to only look at it that way is inherently limiting. And not very creative, I might add.

POST-POLITICAL and the Idea that Government CAN Be Made Better

I am going to separate the working institutions of government from the political industry that has grown around it — for a moment. The political industry produces a multimedia theater that spends billions of dollars every year. The Angertainers are getting paid by the fight, and what they both, Team Red and Team Blue, say is that government cannot be made better. At least, that's what the very loudest and most partisan of our partisanship producers and actors are shouting.

The right says that our government can't be made better, so it advocates across-the-board spending cuts. That point of view has it half right and all wrong. Half right because it recognizes that we cannot financially sustain the spending path we're on. We would be passing a crushing debt load onto our children, and mostly likely their children as well. But too many on Team Red have it all wrong because it doesn't believe that government can be a very valuable tool at all.

I reject that. I like government. Actually, I really love government when it is innovative and responsive. And I've had enough experience with government to know that there is plenty there that is working. But "things that are working" doesn't exactly lead the evening news, does it? It's not Angertainment. In fact, I've been known to really upset my friends in the public sector when I tell them I would *love* to use performance bonuses, so we can really celebrate where government is working. Give me, Citizen Nate, the same or better public service and save me a million tax dollars? Please, take $50,000 for you and your family. Please.

But many members of Team Blue also argue (though it may not recognize that it's doing so) that government cannot be made better. Defending the status quo, staunchly defending old designs in times of change, is also a way of dishonoring the tool of government. I reject that. And I know enough about government to know that there is plenty there that is *not* working. One does not honor government by defending the tool, rather than the outcome. The shame of it is that the Blue Team understands that where there is no functional government, there is chaos and danger. You do not want to live in a place without government. Ask the citizens of Somalia, for instance.

Post-political is not the "purple" politics that mysteriously exists in the ether between Red and Blue — although I happen to be radically moderate in my politics. Post-political is a mind-set and the belief in the ability to respond to our challenges beyond merely passing laws with a heavy bias toward legal regulation. We honor ourselves in the marketplace when we look at the habitats that we have created over time. More and more people on this planet are living longer lives, and more and more are not dying in sickness or by violence. It may not seem like it when you turn on the news, but it's factually true. This is something to celebrate, right?

True, it isn't all roses out there. There are, and always have been, great tragedies to address. We are witnessing conflict, war, and famine throughout our world. It is shocking.

We can wring our hands. Or we can start designing.

Post-political is not the "purple" politics that mysteriously exists in the ether between Red and Blue. Post-political is a mind-set and the belief in the ability to respond to our challenges beyond merely passing laws with a heavy bias toward legal regulation.

Post-political is a necessary mind-set when designing regulations by the creation of cultural habitats. It's not only because we have to get past looking at ourselves in the binary Red versus Blue. We also have to rid ourselves of oppositional thinking as a conflict between business versus labor, environment versus economic health, religion versus religion, and even my [insert issue] versus your [insert issue]. Nothing trumps anything in a post-political world because in that world, it's not about scoring political points in a reality TV series. It's about aligning interests to produce better public outcomes. Post-political is a different focus. It's certainly a wider lens.

We've got some big challenges ahead of ourselves. Let's not blow it.

WAR or TRADE?

WE'RE NEAR THE CONCLUSION, but not the end. This book has been designed to be part of an ongoing conversation. It doesn't pretend to have all the answers — given the dilemmas we face and we've discussed, it shouldn't. But it has been designed to influence, and to help you become more influential in your conversations and actions in building the common good.

Rather than answers, I've offered a framework from which to understand and gain perspective on how we should think about what is truly important to our communities — beyond the current hype and anger. And with that renewed focus, I've offered some thinking as to how and where we can engage in the activity of constructing more prosperous and successful communities. There are many of you out there who, not only are practicing that, but you're leaving me in the dust. Good for you! To bring us full circle to the beginning of this book: If we can think differently and gather differently, we can begin to design differently. And it is definitely time to (re)design, isn't it?

The design of influence centers on intention, not dominance. As an influencer, you probably have a vision; and often, you might become a leader of a group, seeking to develop a common-good solution. If you're on that path, I encourage you not to dominate the conversation and direction, however tempting that may be. Instead, lead from a position of collaboration. Indeed, if you give away your ideas, you'll be pleasantly surprised by how far your relationships can travel and how others can make your good ideas into great ideas.

If our communities are to truly prosper, what we need is not war, but trade. War builds up one side at the expense of the other. Trade builds up all sides, and allows more of us to prosper.

All this is very different from the kind of influence that the Outrage Industry seeks to have. Leave the dominating game to the Angertainers, fear-mongering advocates, and their supporters and financial backers who seek to crush their opponents. I suspect that each side in the battle for intellectual and emotional control over the public sphere knows that their opponents will never be completely crushed — there will always be right and left. Perhaps they prefer that state of permanent warfare to actual out-and-out victory. As we've noted earlier, the Outrage Industry perpetuates itself by being solution-adverse. If any side were to "win," the Outrage Industrialists would have to close up shop. In a way, that should encourage us in our work as designers and influencers — the Angertainers and the Outrage Industry will never be able to dominate the common-good conversation.

Let me repeat: With few exceptions, most of the people toiling in the Outrage Industry are well-intentioned, good people. It's the *design* that is mostly responsible for our current angry mood and inability to make progress in our common challenges. Since the

1930s, we've grown an enormously powerful tool in the form of government. But with that tool's many accomplishments, we have allowed it to crowd out many other alternatives.

What this book argues is that if our communities are to truly prosper, what we need is not war, but trade. War is zero-sum: One side wins, the other loses — or the losers are at least defeated, dominated, and ruled over. War builds up one side at the expense of the other. Trade builds up *all* sides, and allows more of us to prosper. Earlier, I used the Classical Roman forum as a metaphor for those common spaces where citizens can gather to discuss how to build up the common good and improve our communities. Though these days we use the term forum to describe a place where ideas are exchanged, the Roman forums were originally places of economic trade. Forums existed because the communities that gave rise to them understood, consciously or unconsciously, that everyone had something distinctive to offer, and that no one person, tribe, or country was self-sufficient.

War, by contrast, is fundamentally isolationist. And an isolationist community is what the Outrage Industry wishes to perpetuate. In that industry's vision, outsiders have nothing to offer; in fact, they are dangerous to us. *They* are a threat to our most cherished notions. To be open to *their* ideas threatens the very core of our identity. So, we must defend our identities through warfare — mostly through rhetoric and legislation, though in some extreme cases, we'll use terroristic threats and even actual weapons.

But the fact is, whether we like it or not, *they* are *us*. And though many people find excitement, stimulation, and comfort in the self-righteousness of their outrage, more and more people are wearying of this mentality. They want to have greater and more direct involvement in their communities — and that means *everyone* who lives in those communities.

So, how will we come together? What are our forums, our common places? Determining and designing them will require us to move beyond a spectator mentality in our communities. We must cease to be passive consumers of government and information. We must become actors — in other words, we must rediscover the notion of being citizens, and citizens who are defined by more than our votes. We need to rediscover the discipline of *civics*, of civic involvement, and use our influence every day when we make choices on whom to convene with, what to buy, whom to support, and on and on. This is a 24/7 responsibility and opportunity, not something that comes just on the first Tuesday in November.

This responsibility and opportunity will require us to be more empathetic, or at least sympathetic, to our fellow citizens — indeed, to see them as fellow citizens, neighbors, and collaborators on this grand journey. At the very least, it will require us to drop our hubris and our righteous thinking that "our" side has cornered the market on wisdom.

Only by doing this can we reduce the dominance of the Outrage Industry on our public discourse, and in our communities. While I don't care to argue the point that the Outrage Industry should disappear altogether (and that's hardly likely to happen), we can make great headway just by getting rid of the vacuum in which it exists. The Angertainers have power only if we cede the entire field of play to them. By building alternatives, we create the opportunity to think, act, and produce differently.

For the most part, we have a head start, because very few would argue against the Naked Eight threads of a healthy community. From that point of agreement, it becomes easier to start designing and building products and services that aim to address one or more of those arenas. We complete the circle exercising our influence through our networks via the Seven C's. If you want it designed, then you better be prepared to support it.

In a networked world, we don't belong to just one community. We are nodes of interconnection between the people we know

Civics

through our family, our neighborhoods, our friendships, our workplaces, and our passions and activities. So, what are your communities? What do you care most deeply about? How can you facilitate the trade, not only of products and services, but also of ideas and different perspectives and experiences? How can each of us interconnect these networks together for the betterment of us all?

To answer these questions — and they never stay answered — requires the realization that communities are interdependent, and that to prosper from the interdependence requires cooperation, collaboration, listening, and give and take. All this requires each of us to be mindful: to cultivate a self-understanding that habituates us to think critically about ourselves and our opinions, and not just apply that critical thinking to the ideas of others.

This isn't a prescription for utopia. The sixteenth century English philosopher and statesman Thomas More coined the word "utopia" as an ironic pun, from the Greek words *eutopos*, meaning "good place;" and *outopos*, meaning "no place." The ideal world will never exist. Even as we engage in trade across neighborhoods and networks, there will be tensions, and those tensions will never disappear. Indeed, there would be no progress without those tensions, those differences. But that's not the same as saying that war is inevitable. By designing how we influence each other, we can (as much as possible) make those tensions be the engine of a better world, not a *perfect* world — a *better* world, one with the capability of continuous betterment.

 If you want it designed, then you better be prepared to support it.

This is why the challenges we face in our communities are dilemmas. They'll never be solved, because we live in a diverse society, with diverse points of view and ideas. And we'll never have our own way. Only in the political fantasies of the Outrage Industry is this possible — only in those dreams, can we imagine ourselves living in the gated communities of our minds. And let's not kid ourselves. There is always the unknown. Even when we progress toward better designs, we will inevitably find something else that needs to be addressed.

This book doesn't argue that we as citizens can or should "bypass" government. Clearly, that's not only impossible, it's not remotely desirable. Government entities also will remain necessary tools. Except glancingly, we haven't addressed the great perpetual dilemma of how large a role government should have in its citizens' welfare — in other words, how "big" or "small" government should be. How much should government policy and funding be involved in issues, such as the development of new forms of transportation and energy, health care and old-age insurance, and so on?

Actually, those might not even be the right questions. Rather, shouldn't we be asking where the tool of government could produce the most value? And the greater point is that if government is to be truly valuable, it needs to be used in combination with other institutional forms in our society.

And even at that, we should first ask ourselves this: How are we addressing the imperatives of those Naked Eight strands that support us? With an outcomes-orientation rather than an output of putting points on the board, we should find additional tools to weigh in on those challenges. Slashing government isn't a design; it's a tactic. Building something that works well in its stead, so that we release ourselves of continually having to go back to the government tool, is the way to keep our eye on the important things — that is, those issues involving the Naked Eight. That, by the way, is not just a prescription for more effective societal results. It will also restore much needed confidence that we should — indeed, need to have — in our governmental institutions.

It is clear that we simply cannot afford to continually design the common good by warring over how little or how much government to throw at a challenge. And as I've argued, that's not just a statement on our inability to financially sustain our current relationship with government. We simply can't allow ourselves to be that *uncreative*. We need to have a new relationship with our communities and creatively design using every tool at our disposal: every technology, every institution, and every different way of thinking. And it all starts with a mind-set. It may strike you as simple to the point of being so obvious that it seems irrelevant. But agreeing to start where we agree — around the Naked Eight — is actually incredibly relevant. Stripped naked, these common challenges are what bind us together; it is where we begin to apply all of the tools at our disposal.

We simply cannot afford to continually design the common good by warring over how little or how much government to throw at a challenge.

One of the wonderful things about this opportunity is that you don't have to feel like you have to be a leader on each and every issue: just pick something. A dramatic impact of our newly-networked world is that it has created an influencers society. Pick just about any issue and somewhere around one in ten is telling the other nine where to eat, what movies to see, what to buy, how to vote, where to travel, and on and on. Most everyone has an interest and a reputation, i.e., the ability to influence others on one subject or another. In other words, you don't have to upend everything in your life and start feeling guilty about what you're not doing. Have fun and find meaning in doing something: From the anyone to the many ones is how we'll move forward.

We have never, ever succeeded with intolerance. We have never thrived when we have practiced religious, racial, or sexual intolerance. In a nation founded on a set of civic ideals, what could be more damaging than to be philosophically intolerant about how we go about addressing our common challenges? In an ever-changing

(m)any

world, can there be a greater danger than to punch at each other with self-assured dogma?

I don't have all the solutions and I don't pretend to. This isn't the last word.

But I do honestly hope that I had some influence on you.

Thank you for that opportunity. Now it's your turn to influence me.

You Seem Too Optimistic. Are You on Something?

Yes, I'm on something ... the same path that I've been on for decades: building better communities. A number of years ago, I gave a speech with the pithy title of <u>Uncivil Discourse and the Rise of the Outrage Industry</u> where I pointed out how we had commoditized anger in our society. We are literally selling anger. Well, there's a great adage that states the first cure to a disease is to name it. I'm not angry. Not at all. I'm purposed and my experiences have shown me over and over that I have reason to feel purpose and optimism. I have two young daughters. I have dear friends with children. We have a world that needs to be handed off to them. It's not a perfect world, but it is largely a better world than at any time prior. I'm not interested in passing the baton of hopelessness and anger. What kind of hand off is that? Here, have this piece of crap that you can't fix anyway. What kind of gift is that?

STANDING ON THE SHOULDERS OF GIANTS

Creativity and innovation are the products of trade, not of war.

If you've ever spent some time navigating the pages of the Brain Pickings website (www.brainpickings.org) — one of the most stimulating collections of cultural ideas out there today — you've likely gathered that its overarching theme is creativity. The people behind this site believe that creativity isn't a supernatural force, but a *combinatorial force*, or a combination of new ideas with pre-existing ones.

When it comes to designing our common-good habitats, collaborative creation is key. Applying new, cutting-edge ideas to the foundation of original ideas leads to incredible technologies, even though at first it may seem that the two ideas couldn't produce something greater than the sum of each part. By taking a look at the way old neighborhoods and communities were structured and combining it with progressive thinking, you'll find new great inventions, like vertical gardens or wind turbines,

It also may seem to some that creative collaboration is unjust, because ideas are being pulled from various sources. But this type of combinational thinking is the reason we have the technology, the art, and the music that we have today. Apple, for example, didn't come up with the idea of a desktop computer on its own — founders Steve Jobs and Steve Wozniak borrowed from Xerox's existing technology. What Apple did was take the idea into new and more useful directions. We can think of it more in terms of standing on the shoulders of giants than stealing ideas from others. The important thing is to always remember our creativity, though seemingly supernatural, is little more than the application of our ideas to those already in existence.

What projects are you working on, so you can be a giant to future innovators?

What's Grabbing Your Attention
These Days?

ONE OF THE BEST WAYS TO START trading is by sharing information. And in that vein, I'd be remiss if I didn't point you to some of the platforms and people that I find interesting in this space. It's quite obvious that this is hardly an exhaustive listing of sites that are serving as hubs of socially-innovative products and services. And it's equally so that the folks whom I'm following are not everyone you could or would find interesting. This is merely a sampling of what and whom I'm paying attention to. Check it out and let me know what you think. And tell me who and what is piquing your interest as well. Please.

Not surprisingly, there's plenty out there in the world of environmental design. Here are a few leads to get you started.

- ◆ **Environment & Ecosystems:**
  - ▪ **Sustainability is Good:**
    www.sustainableisgood.com/blog
    - ▫ Forum for sustainable packaging, design and living that uses 100 percent renewable energy.
  - ▪ **Ecopreneurist:** http://ecopreneurist.com
    - ▫ A resource for eco-minded entrepreneurs that gives them access to information to make their businesses more eco-friendly.
  - ▪ **Environmental Leader:**
    www.environmentalleader.com
    - ▫ Online portal for information on energy efficiency and sustainable leadership.
  - ▪ **Amazon Green:**
    www.amazon.com/AmazonGreen/b?ie=UTF8&node=394379011
    - ▫ This website has tips for living green and links to all its eco-friendly, sustainable living, organic, and green products.
  - ▪ **The Green Thing:**
    www.dothegreenthing.com
    - ▫ This website explains seven different ways to live greener lives. It has a blog about being green, and an online store to purchase green products.

In chapter six, I wrote about how we really have a sick care system, rather than a health care system, designed to keep you healthy, rather than repairing you once you're out of sorts. Here are a few sites that will give you the tools to start operating with that mind-set.

- ◆ **Health & Wellness:**
  - ▪ **Organic Lifestyle Magazine:**
    www.organiclifestylemagazine.com

- ▫ A magazine focused on healthy alternatives, eating organic, and staying active.
- ■ **iTunes Health & Fitness:**
  http://itunes.apple.com/us/genre/ios-health-fitness/id6013?mt=8
  - ▫ Apps for health and wellness; some are free and some have a small fee.
- ■ **Infinite Wellness Solutions:**
  www.infinitewellnesssolutions.com/interactive.html
  - ▫ A directory of online employee wellness programs, including fitness, alcohol control, and weight loss programs.
- ■ **U.S. Preventative Medicine:**
  www.uspreventivemedicine.com
  - ▫ A one-stop-shop for preventative medicine information, such as videos, downloads, webinars, podcasts, and more.
- ■ **The Prevention Plan:**
  www.thepreventionplan.com
  - ▫ Personalized health management program (that you pay for) and support system.
  - ▫ The Prevention Plan created Macaw, a free health and fitness app: www.uspreventivemedicine.com/Macaw-App/Macaw-App-(1).aspx

What we commonly call education is usually a conversation about the tools that we've created toward the end of passing on knowledge and wisdom. Here are some sites that are pushing the limits of how we can receive ideas in ways that are interesting, useful, and compelling — and free, by the way.

- ◆ **Educational Reform:**
  - ■ **Khan Academy:**

www.khanacademy.org

- ▫ Has a library of 2,700 plus educational videos, covering virtually any topic you'd want to learn.
- **Academic Earth:**

  http://academicearth.org
  - ▫ Offers videos of college lectures on a wide variety of topics and from a wide variety of renowned universities.
- **BrainPop:**

  www.brainpop.com
  - ▫ An educational website for children, covering all topics from arts and music to engineering and technology.
- **Open Culture:**

  www.openculture.com
  - ▫ Offers a bevy of free online courses (on essentially every topic, and many languages), along with access to many free films (including Film Noir, Hitchcock, or John Wayne films).
- **iTunes U:**

  www.apple.com/education/itunes-u
  - ▫ Free university courses you can access on your iPad, iPhone, or iPod.
- **Discovery Education:**

  www.discoveryeducation.com
  - ▫ Online hub of digital content for schools, including webinars, documentaries, and free step-by-step programs for various subjects.

- ◆ **Social Awareness:**
  - **MYOO:**

    http://myoo.com/about

- ◻ Dedicated to sparking innovative change and driving real-world solutions through collaboration.
- **Stanford Social Innovation Review:**
  www.ssireview.org
  - ◻ Articles, books, and blogs about social entrepreneurship.
- **Philadelphia Social Innovations Journal:**
  www.philasocialinnovations.org/site/index.php
  - ◻ Follow this journal to hear about social innovation goings-on.

In my introduction, I mentioned a painfully incomplete list of my teachers. Well, here I get to cheat and add a few more: all interesting folks who are interested in so many, many things. Thanks for letting me follow you.

Nilofer Merchant @nilofer
http://nilofermerchant.com

Andrea Learned @AndreaLearned
http://learnedon.com

Fabian Pattberg @FabianPattberg
www.fabianpattberg.com

Jack Uldrich @jumpthecurve
http://jumpthecurve.net

Scott Belsky @scottbelsky
www.scottbelsky.com

Nell Edgington @nedgington
www.socialvelocity.net

Rachel Greenberger @BusinessForFood
www.babson.edu/Academics/centers/the-lewis-institute/
Pages/food-sol.aspx

Maria Popova @brainpicker
www.brainpickings.org

Jeffrey Hogue @JeffreyHogue

Kelly Groehler @KellyGroehler

Lauren DeWitt @Lauren4Good

David Agus @DavidAgus
http://davidagus.com

Lars Leafblad @larsleafblad
www.minnpost.com/author/lars-leafblad

CecilySommers @cecilysommers

Sharon Ann Lee @CultureBrain
www.culture-brain.com

Andrew Zimmern @andrewzimmern
http://andrewzimmern.com

Chris Guillebeau @chrisguillebeau
http://chrisguillebeau.com

Amber Rae @heyamberrae
http://tumblr.heyamberrae.com

Jenny Evans @powerhousepc

Seth Godin @thisissethsblog
   www.sethgodin.com

Aaron Koblin @aaronkoblin
   www.aaronkoblin.com

Daniel Pink @DanielPink
   www.danpink.com

Hugh McLeod @GapingVoid
   www.gapingvoid.com

I love that these days, we get to admit that there is entertainment value in ideas: millions of hits on hundreds of sites. Here's some that I find myself returning to time and time again.

The 99 Percent
   http://the99percent.com

Harvard Social Enterprise
   www.hbs.edu/socialenterprise

GOOD Magazine
   www.good.is

TED
   www.ted.com

Business Exchange's Social Entrepreneurship
   http://bx.businessweek.com/social-entrepreneurship

The Vine Speaks
> http://thevinespeaks.com

TEDx
> (independently produced TED events from all over the planet. www.ted.com/tedx)

Mashable — Social Good
> http://mashable.com/social-good

Babson's Insight Newsletter (on thought leadership)
> www.babson.edu/executive-education/thought-leadership/babson-insight/Pages/home.aspx

Do Lectures (talks that inspire action)
> www.dolectures.com

PopTech
> http://poptech.org

Center for Social Innovation
> www.center4si.com

Get Resilient
> www.getresilient.com

The Prevention Plan
> www.thepreventionplan.com/Tools/Blog.aspx

Design Intelligence
> www.di.net

The Atlantic Cities

www.theatlanticcities.com

Springwise.com

www.springwise.com

Revolution.Is

http://revolution.is

Grist

http://grist.org

Idea Mensch

http://ideamensch.com

Fast Co. Design

www.fastcodesign.com

INDEX

C

M

N

CPSIA information can be obtained at www.ICGtesting.com
Printed in the USA
BVOW070414240113

311225BV00001B/1/P

9 780985 592608